Leadership 6-S

How to Love Them and Lead Them with Empathy

Vera Jones

In memory of William T. and Mary K. Jones, who taught me many great lessons—the greatest being how much they cared.

To Dr. Jan Bethea, who, with a decade of persistent insistence, appealed to my sense of Significance to finish this empathic leadership book.

And to every servant leader who embraces EMPATHY as their Superpower—God bless your Significance and Purpose.

Contents

Acknowledgments

I give all praise and glory to God—My Creator. My Father. And I'm grateful for the example of Jesus Christ as the Ultimate Empath!

I thank my son, Andrew Veran Soleyn, who has taught me more lessons in empathy than one can ever imagine. You are my inspirational hero, and I am determined to keep shining light on your strength and your story so you will always know your pain was never in vain.

I am tremendously grateful to Dr. Jan Bethea for insisting I had a leadership book in me, and for always pushing me to get it out into the world. Thank you for being an unwavering best friend.

I thank Dawn Josephson, The Master Writing Coach, who is proof that even coaches need coaches to push them to their best. Thank you for getting this book across the finish line.

Thank you to my V-Team, Michelle and Jela, who are the most supportive and diligent virtual assistants on the planet.

I thank the little grocery store in Bloomington, IN and "Ricky." I may not have remembered your names, but I remembered exactly how you made me feel that one fateful day. Because of you, "I GOT IT" and now, the world does too!

Thank you to the thousands of clients and every organization who has ever participated in a Leadership 6-S training, coaching, keynote, or survey that led me one step closer to truly understanding where empathy meets motivation and why it has the greatest potential to drive each of us to our best.

I thank Karen Young (USPTO), Tom Reber (Cross Country Mortgage), and Kenneth Hannaman (Arby's), who painted avatars for me of what genuine, empathic leadership looks and feels like.

I thank my Leo sister, Dianna, who has always been there when I was the one in need of empathy and poured it out with a heavy hand in a way only a true lioness could understand.

I thank my mother and father, who live on in heaven now, but whose spirits have never left me, and have always encouraged me to encourage others.

To my love, Levert, my brother, DJ, and my cherished small circle of close family and friends, thank you for just loving me for crazy me.

Introduction

What motivates you to do what you do? What drives you to your best? For many, these are simple questions yet difficult to answer. I've always thought about work in terms of what I did or didn't enjoy about a specific duty or task. But I never really thought about what drove me to be my best or what motivated me to go above and beyond during moments of adversity or lethargy. As I got older and hopefully wiser, I realized that most people struggle to conceptualize or articulate their impetus for motivation. In fact, about 80% of the people I coached, trained, or just randomly asked in conversation did not concretely know the answer to these motivational questions.

My "aha" moment came shortly after my mother suddenly died from a heart attack in March of 2007. It was one of only a handful of times that I struggled to find motivation of any kind to do anything. I was a single parent to a nine-year-old son in Bloomington, IN, with an elderly father to look after in Jacksonville, FL. I had a lot of responsibilities, yet I just could not find the motivation to engage. I was a former collegiate athlete, a sports analyst, and at the time an assistant coach at Indiana University. I was a sports nut since the age of five. I convinced myself I was one of the fortunate few who, over years of experience, developed the winner's mentality that helps one play through life's fouls. But I had never experienced adversity and pain like this in all my days of competitive sports. Depression proved to be an extremely formidable opponent.

One fateful day soon after my mother's funeral, I visited a small grocery store where a cognitively disabled young man, who I named Ricky, assisted me. That experience set the example for me of what true engagement and resilience look like. It helped me understand that there was an emotional nudge in all of us to push through inevitable moments of lack of engagement and motivation. That day I learned leadership lessons, witnessed the true power of empathy, and embraced the power of words and perspectives like I had never experienced before. It's surreal that on that day, when I was so entrenched and self-absorbed in pain and confusion, that I could have allowed an empathetic experience to blossom into an entire leadership theory, book, and training transformation.

I learned that despite our challenges or adversity, at any given moment, the right words of encouragement, the right direction, and the right amount of caring or compassion could accomplish amazing results. I should have already known this because it had happened to me many times on the basketball court. Good coaching and leadership over the years often helped me achieve things I had at one time only dreamed of accomplishing. This experience, however, was more divinely evident. I soon deeply embraced the power of words, and how the right words spoken from a caring heart could change a life, because it was my life that was changing. Through this transformation, I found my true calling to help coach, inspire, lead, and transform others.

Just two weeks before my mother passed away, she offered me the most left-field advice I had ever received. "You need to give up basketball," she matter-of-factly stated one evening. "I know you've loved it since you were a little girl. But you're missing your calling. What you need to do is finish writing that book and get yourself on the speaker's circuit so you can inspire people. Then you can get yourself on Oprah." (My mother absolutely loved Oprah!)

As odd and unprecedented as this felt in that March Madness moment, it all began to come into fruition for me in waves of thoughts during and after my grocery store experience. That moment was the birthing of an entirely new entrepreneurial career of purpose and prophecy for me. It was also the birthing of the thought leadership behind this book. I was learning how emotion, words, and empathy could motivate us in our personal and professional lives. I was becoming the living example of just how much so. I was finding the answers to what motivates us to do what we do, what drives us to our best, and in adverse times, how empathic leadership and communication help. It took another fateful moment—a "bad boss" experience—and thousands of inquisitive conversations and surveys over the course of almost a decade before I truly understood how it all applied to the workplace and the universal engagement needed for maximum productivity.

Generic research reveals that at our human core we are motivated by power, achievement, and belonging. We know that fear and pain are very strong but negative and unpredictable motivators too. It is fair to say our motivations are as unique as we are and as varied as our experiences. In the workplace, where leaders are held highly responsible for the engagement and morale of their teams, expecting them to exert the cognitive energy and time to learn all the nuances of behavior, attitudes, backgrounds, and values that exist in the world, in an attempt to understand every employee, is as unreasonable as it is impossible. Yet, this is what we have done for decades, leaving leaders at a loss for how to motivate simply and effectively, let alone where empathy is supposed to fit into the leadership picture. Until now. Until Leadership 6-S.

This book will introduce you to six core workplace motivators that, by design, begin with the letter "S." It is by design, because when you put "6" and "S" together, you get "Success!" (You will soon learn I speak "clever" and "sarcasm" fluently.) That is my desire for you—to achieve leadership success! I wrote this book to help you understand that in the workplace, we all, to varying degrees, are motivated by Significance, Security, Solutions, Structure, Sincerity, and Selflessness. When you learn how to relate to others within these six S-Motivators, you grow your ability to lead with improved connection, communication, and collaboration. And you will do it with greater self-awareness, empathy, and confidence in your leadership ability.

People crave leaders who "get" them—not just who they are, but what they care about and what motivates and drives them to achieve. When leaders put their energy and empathy into these motivations, they ultimately find the key to engagement and productivity so many workplaces lack. As one who now embraces my Significance motivation, I'm proud of this book, because I am excited about its impactful potential for your leadership legacy. I did not always know my leadership potential. But thank God my mother did, and her empathic words led me to manifest this book in your possession. I pray you use it to become what the world needs more of—an empathic leader. And I trust you will become a leader that is far greater than you ever imagined. It is time you learn just how Significant you are, and that you will grow even more in your Significance every time you empathically empower others to believe in theirs!

CHAPTER 1

LEADERSHIP – WHAT IS IT ANYWAY?

> *"Leadership is about empathy. It is about having the ability to relate to and connect with people for the purpose of inspiring and empowering their lives."*
> —*Oprah Winfrey*

What is the first image that comes to mind when you think of great leadership? Is it the image of a notable historic figure, like Abraham Lincoln, Mother Teresa, Nelson Mandela, Mahatma Gandhi, or Martin Luther King, Jr.? Or does your mental canvas feature a more current personality, like a social media influencer or business mogul? For many, the image could be more intimate, such as a parent, grandparent, or sports coach. Others may visualize a teacher, mentor, or religious figure. Some may even think of a supervisor or organizational leader. Reflect on that first image that surfaced. Did you feel a sense of satisfaction or admiration? Perhaps you smiled as you reflected on the impact such leadership had on your life.

Conversely, what is the first image that comes to mind when you think of poor leadership? Did you once again conjure the image of a person? Or, this time, did you think of the detrimental impact the poor leadership had on you or others? Did you feel your mood shift? Perhaps you sighed, rolled your eyes, twisted your lips, or shook your head in disapproving judgment?

Leadership, whether you deem it good or bad, can evoke emotional and even physical responses, simply upon recall and reflection. No wonder most new leaders desperately want to be good at it. Even current leaders whom many would deem "good" often fear that people will disapprove of their leadership skills. Some even self-sabotage their leadership efforts as they allow their fear, rather than their confidence and courage, to drive them.

Recently, while I was coaching one of my closest friends and colleagues, I saw firsthand how prevalent this fear is. Dr. J is someone I greatly respect and believe to be a great leader. She is a college professor in sports management, where effective leadership is not only taught but also critically required. She revealed that she felt uneasy about receiving a negative end-of-the-year review from one of her students. I asked if she had received many negative reviews. "No," she lamented. "My overall reviews were positive. It's just this one that bothers me. I think it came from the student I had to give a failing grade, but I can't be sure since the reviews are anonymous." To recap, overall, her reviews were positive. Just one negative review was enough to cause her tremendous disappointment and concern. Dr. J reminded me how little it takes for many of us to fear we are somehow failing as a leader.

If you have ever had to suffer under poor leadership, then chances are that when it's time for you to lead, you want to be better. Most people fear so much simply because they care so much to get it right. After all, other people's lives, futures, personal and professional development, and psychological memories are at stake. Even you, reading this, are here because you care.

I recognize that we all care about our own development and futures too, including our reputation and vocational security. So, yes, there is a selfish interest, especially for type-A perfectionists. (It's okay to admit if you are one. You're in good company. Been there … did that. I promise that this is a no-judgment zone.)

Today, I invite you to dig deeper—to go to that place where humanity reigns, emotional intelligence rules, and humility resides. It is that place within you that cares about others in a way that makes you desire to see and feel things from their perspective. If you've found that place, then you are already on your way to becoming a great leader, because caring is at the core of empathy. This book will help you grow in that space of learning to engage others empathically. You'll discover how to make the relational connections that make others feel significance and that contribute to your success as a leader.

A New Mindset

To begin this leadership journey, you must adopt the mindset that I insist all my coaching students, colleagues, and clients develop and implement. If you want to overcome adversity, you must be willing to drop some F-Bombs. Before you judge me, I'm not talking about the potty-mouth expletives that occasionally fly out when someone cuts you off in traffic. The F-Bombs I'm referring to are Fear, Fouls, and Failure. Drop these thoughts and be ready to replace them with Faith, Focus, and Fortitude. To do this and to develop as an empathic leader, remember to ***focus on being IMPROVED, not approved.***

When your focus is on being ***approved***, you set yourself up for fear of judgment. *"Do they think I'm smart enough, good enough, experienced enough?"* you ask. The adversity you face, what I call fouls, becomes insurmountable and psychologically painful to process because even when you make simple mistakes, your fear of judgment magnifies and distorts how bad things really are. Failure then becomes your focus and eventually your reality as you tumble headfirst into the negativity trap.

In contrast, when your focus is on being ***improved***, you find the faith to believe you can do better in some way. Your curiosity gets stimulated to learn new approaches, and you focus on that positive pursuit. You willingly find the fortitude to accept your mistakes and challenges, because your true end game is to be your best to serve others.

When I was a young leader, I took criticism to heart, and I beat myself up excessively. I learned the hard way how to adopt this "improved, not approved" mentality, and it has served me, and subsequently others I've led and coached, quite well over the years. As you navigate through this book, keep an open mind to the wonderful ways you will be challenged to grow in self-awareness and emotional intelligence, two key components in developing as an empathic leader. The courage and humility required to take an honest look into who you are and how you relate with others is the same courage and humility that will grant you the confidence and compassion necessary to become an empathic leader—the great one you desire to be, and the one the world needs you to be!

The 6 Ws of Leadership

Let's explore "leadership" with a deep dive into the 6 Ws:

- **Who?** As I demonstrated with my initial questions, our minds tend to focus on a specific person when we hear the word "leader" or "leadership." Since 65-70 percent of people are visual in recall or cognitive tendency, a "who" is usually the first image that comes to mind. In other words, we often think of leadership by imagining a person with a title or position of prominence or authority: a boss, the President, a head coach, a priest or minister, the principal, a CEO, or a company founder. In short, we see the "who" as the "the person in charge."

- **What?** This is typically the next thing we assign to leadership. We think about what the leader does, the tasks they complete, or the people they lead. Most dictionaries define leadership as one with an office or position of influencing, guiding, directing, coaching, managing, ruling, governing, molding, overseeing, or basically "running things."

- **When?** Most people think of a leader as someone who leads every day or in some consistent capacity. Hence, the "when" has its place in leadership. In times of conflict, challenge, and uncertainty is when we need and seek leadership the most. The famous quote from Martin Luther King, Jr. comes to mind: ***"The ultimate measure of a man is not where he stands in moments of convenience and comfort, but where he stands at times of challenge and controversy."*** When things are going well, we often overlook our need for leaders. We tend to self-lead or self-manage when all is right with the world.

- **Where?** We tend to think of leaders when and where we most need them. While at times leaders are consciously invisible to us, they are indeed everywhere. We have leaders in government, at our jobs, in businesses, on our teams, in our schools, in social groups, and in religious places. In the animal kingdom, inherent in nature, packs and flocks establish their own hierarchy with a prevailing leader. Even mother nature herself gets a nod for power and authority.

- **Why?** Because leadership is so innate, the following question may be the most important but least thought about: "Why do people follow leaders?" Think about it. Do people follow you because you know more, are the most skilled, are the boss's son or daughter, have 20 years seniority in the company? Did someone tell people to follow you, or did you volunteer to lead? Regardless of why you THINK they follow you, the fact is, fundamentally, *people follow you based on how they see ("C") you*—your Character, Communication and Choices.

The great debate as to whether the ability to lead is something people are born with or something they learn resides here. My answer is that it is both. Some people have seemingly innate personality traits that encompass strong communication skills and character attributes. Because of these character attributes, they tend to make wise choices. However, character, communication, and choices are all things people can develop within themselves too. Think of why you tend to follow people. Can you see these things?

- o *Character* – There are values and character traits you naturally align with, admire, and respect. Of those, a few more "C's" generally top the list: confidence, courage, competence, charisma, and compassion. Integrity usually gets a big nod as well. The adage of "birds of a feather flock together" is typically true, so the person who demonstrates the core values of a group emerges or is voted in as the leader and helps to design and perpetuate a culture. Conflict and detraction often arise when others are not aligned with the leader's character or the greater culture that leader represents.
- o *Communication* – We know that what you say and how you say it are basic keys of communication. People need leaders to

communicate a wide variety of things that drive them, such as inspiration, knowledge, solutions, and concern for their wellbeing and the greater good. I like to teach my empathic communication theory called "The Catch" as one of the most powerful mindsets you can master as a communicator.

Let's suppose that you want to toss a ball with a friend. You (the sender) ask your friend (the receiver) if they wish to play catch with you. Assuming your friend is the fun and energetic type, you receive a resounding "yes." You then toss over the ball (the message). Your friend catches it. Did you communicate? Yes, because the ball was caught. The message was received. Now, the next time you throw the ball to your friend, they drop it. Did you communicate? No, because the ball dropped. The message was NOT received. Knowing this, what is the most critical part of the communication process? If you said "the catch," you're right! The process of communication is incomplete without receipt of the message.

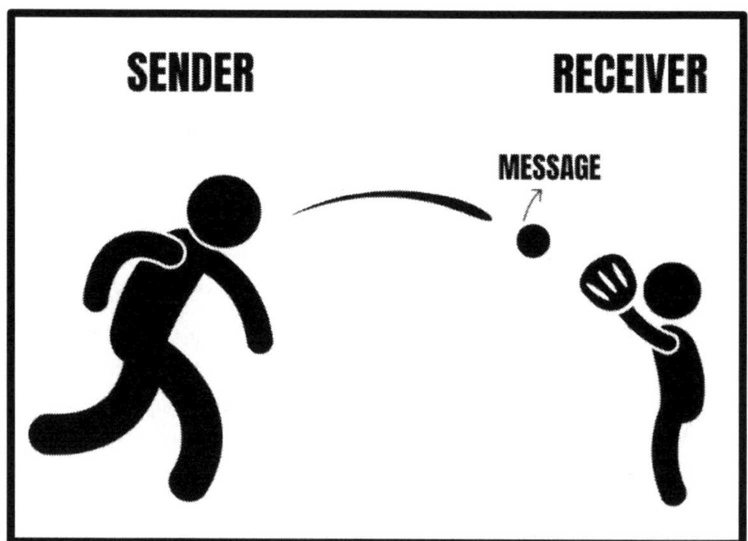

The most important point for you to grasp is this: No matter how important, fabulous, or game-changing your message is, if your recipient doesn't catch or receive it, the message is meaningless.

Therefore, the onus of communication is on the person initiating the ball toss. You must make sure you are sending your message in a way that others can receive it.

Suppose your friend says, "I can only catch the ball when you throw it at my chest area or higher. I have a bad back and cannot bend." Would you then roll the ball? Of course not, because you know the pass will not get caught. Equally important, you *care* enough about the bad back situation to not make matters worse. This is my simple visual analogy for empathic communication. You communicate and lead based on who is catching the ball and how they can best receive what you are throwing, not solely because you just want or need to throw it.

One of the greatest problems in leadership resides in the lack of empathic communication. Leaders need things done effectively, efficiently, and expeditiously. As such, many people tend to not focus on the catch and to just throw the ball any way that suits them at a given moment. Sometimes they throw too hard, too high, too low, too fast, too short, or too soft. That's when the ball gets dropped. Do this often enough and eventually people do not want to play catch with you. A little more empathic attention to how the receiver is best prepared to play catch with you can be the difference between people following you with great commitment and enthusiasm or not.

o   *Choices* – People are most interested in following you when they see how your choices could somehow benefit them. Even in something as simplistic as choosing to go to a public restroom, a leadership situation emerges. We see it all the time at social events. One woman says, "I'm going to the restroom." Another says, "Oh, you know where it is? I'll follow you!" Instant leadership!

Of course, the leadership issues we deal with in the workplace are far more complex, but this example speaks volumes for how quickly your choices can make a difference in whether people will choose to follow you or not. Just like with character and communication, when people see that what you do or say aligns with or benefits their wants and needs, they are more open to following your lead.

- **How?** Finally, we arrive at the **big question of "how."** While the "why" is most overlooked, the "how" is the most asked. "How do I effectively lead?" Countless models, processes, and formulas for leadership exist, and we have a plethora of experts who boldly tackle this question. One of my best recommendations (and favorite exercises with my clients and groups) is to first learn about and assess your leadership style. To do so, I point people in the direction of Daniel Goleman's Leadership Styles.

Psychologist Daniel Goleman, Ph.D., is the author of several books about emotional intelligence and leadership. In his book *Primal Leadership* (2001), Dr. Goleman and co-authors Richard Boyatzis and Annie McKee revealed six leadership styles. Once you learn your own go-to styles or leadership strengths, you should also learn what styles you need to develop and what situations will work best to apply each of them.

According to Goleman, there are four leadership styles that best resonate with people because of the degree of empathy and emotional intelligence that drive them. Those four styles are the affiliative, democratic, authoritative, and coaching styles. The pacesetting and coercive leadership styles are more of what I call "old-school, do as I say right now" styles. (Enter tearful and fearful flashbacks of my parents on any given week when I didn't clean my room or wash the dishes.) These two styles have their place, but only in very specific leadership situations, as they are not geared towards empathy. I include a summary of each style below, as I think it will help answer the pressing question of, "How do I effectively lead?" Note how character, communication, and choices are reflected in each.

The Affiliative Leader

The *Affiliative* leader is characterized as one who **prioritizes people** by valuing their well-being, abilities, and needs. They are strong, empathic communicators who create emotional bonds and harmony for relationship building. They communicate **"people first"** and may say, *"Tell me how you feel."* This style is best applied when there is a need for team motivation or conflict resolution. It is a very people-oriented style and least focused on completing specific tasks or goals other than relationship building that moves people forward. This is not the style that chooses to get things done in a hurry, but rather chooses to diminish worry by taking the time to unify teams and motivate people to feel significant and secure.

The Democratic Leader

The *Democratic* leader is characterized as one who **prioritizes collaboration** and getting people to share ideas and opinions to arrive at workable agreements. They communicate with empathy and inclusiveness, asking questions like *"What do you think?"* This style chooses to work towards unity and building a culture of agreement and accountability. But due to the time it takes for obtaining consensus, it does not guarantee rapid delivery of tasks, projects, or solutions.

The Coaching Leader

The *Coaching* leader is characterized as one who **prioritizes individual development** and focuses on improving people's knowledge and skillsets. They communicate with high levels of motivation, knowledge, and empathy in understanding the developmental needs and abilities of teammates or staff members. They may say, *"Let's try it,"* and they may use a variety of approaches to help people try new ideas, processes, or tactics to help people accomplish goals. This style is the choice when the leader and the organization see the value of placing a commitment in the long-term development of its team members.

The Visionary Leader

The **Visionary, also known as the Authoritative** leader, is characterized as one who **prioritizes the big picture**, setting the stage for the highest levels of achievement. This leader communicates, **"Come with me,"** and displays confidence, inspiration, positivity, and future to engage people to buy into the vision, direction, and objectives of an organization or team. This style encourages innovation, creativity, and motivation, most useful in new or change-management scenarios. These visionary leaders choose to focus on setting up clear directives for what's needed for future growth and opportunity.

The Pacesetter Leader

The **Pacesetter** leader is characterized as one who **prioritizes efficient, self-direction.** This is a task-focused style that communicates a need for high-drive, grit, and excellence. They are quick to say, **"Do as I do, now"** or **"Follow my example."** They are fast initiators who want to show others how it's done then quickly get them to accomplish the task on their own. This style of leadership is not effective when people need detail, instruction, or time to develop. It is more effective in leading highly competent, skilled, and motivated team members. This leader chooses to lead by example, typically in fast-paced scenarios. This style cannot be sustained for a long period of time as worker burnout is common.

The Coercive Leader

The Coercive leader is characterized as one who **prioritizes immediate obedience** to direction and command. This leadership style communicates, **"Do as I say, right now"** with no-nonsense, militancy, authority, and power. This leader is highly driven, goal-oriented, self-controlled, and self-directed. Typically used in crisis situations, where there is no time for individual disagreement or democracy, this leadership style makes a choice that insists upon single authority and immediate compliance. This "no questions asked," style of leadership is the least empathic, and can have a very negative impact on how people feel and relate, and therefore cannot be relied upon as a reliable style of leadership for a consistently, long period of time.

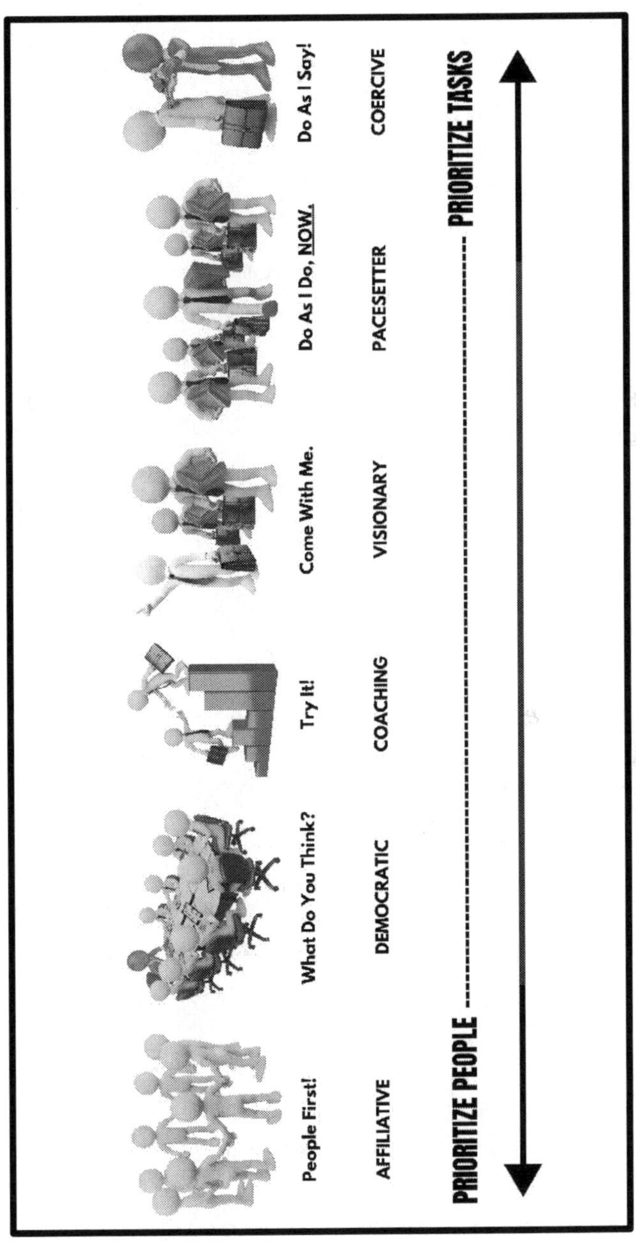

Show Them You Care

As you can see, each leadership style has its place depending on the current scenario and needs. Developing yourself in all styles will help broaden your versatility to lead in diverse situations. However, the more empathic styles, (affiliate, democratic, coaching, and authoritative) will best equip leaders who want to grow in their ability to lead with relationship and emotional substance. These four styles place the emphasis on connecting, collaborating, and developing people. They encourage leaders to pay attention to individual needs and motivations to achieve, as that's what people want and need most from leadership. Remember, people are always evaluating you through what you say and do. Your character, communication, and choices are always on display and are the fundamental bridge for connecting *WHY* people will follow you to *HOW* you should respond with leadership.

Ultimately, if you want to be a great leader, the biggest C to master is to CARE! And that's really what this book is all about. All the Ws and all the Cs considered, your leadership legacy will be summed up by how much people perceived that you cared about them. When people feel cared for, they will follow you and do the best they can to move the organization forward.

Caring is at the heart of empathic leadership, which means you are always guiding, coaching, training, moving, advising, and motivating each person by considering *their* needs, perspectives, and abilities. Each employee you lead is made up of emotions and has specific motivational needs to be met to be their best. You cannot avoid those emotions, no matter how tricky and finicky they can be at times. It's what humans are made of. You must at least CARE about your people even if you do not fully understand them. Your ability to accomplish this is what will set you apart as a great, empathic leader.

Realize that being the boss, manager, supervisor, founder, or executive head person in charge does not automatically make you the leader. As you contemplate the difference between a title and a true leader, remember the famous quote: ***"They don't care how much you know until they know how much you care."*** In today's workplace, more than ever, your followers need more than simply being told what to do. They want you to care about them and their ability to do or not do. Self-awareness and emotional intelligence are the keys that turn on your leadership ignition, and you will soon discover that empathy steers and drives people where they need to go! Once you tap into who you are and what you offer (your style and skillsets as a leader), then you must consistently be open to perspective taking of who others are, what their skillsets are, and what drives them emotionally to do what needs to be done. If that's why you are here, then that is definitely why I am here. It's time for you to be that face of great leadership people envision.

Empathy AAA Exercises

Awareness

- Who are you as a person? As a leader? How do you know?
- What character values are most important to you? Complete the Values Sort Exercise on page 155 to discover.
- What values do you think are most important to your organization? To the people you lead? Consider having your team members self-assess their values, and then compare similarities and differences.

Accountability

- What does good/bad leadership look like to you?
- Who do you want to be as a leader (what values)?
- How will you know you've arrived?
- Who will help to keep you accountable?

Action

- Complete the Perceptions Survey on page 157. What similarities do you find to your self-assessment?
- Take Daniel Goleman's Leadership Styles Quiz. You can find a quick assessment here: https://www.skillsyouneed.com/quiz/325444.

CHAPTER 2

I GOT IT! THE CASE FOR EMPATHY

> *"The path to gaining respect is paved with knowledge and empathy."*
> *–Evan Brown*

I've been tossing around this word "empathy," but what exactly is it? For many people, empathy is simple to conceptualize, yet it isn't always simple to experience. According to Hodges and Myers in the Encyclopedia of Social Psychology, empathy is defined as *understanding another person's experience by imagining oneself in that other person's situation.* A basic version of Merriam Webster's definition states that empathy is *the action of understanding, being aware of, being sensitive to, and vicariously experiencing the feelings, thoughts, and experiences of another.*

Very Well Mind and psychology experts go a bit further and break empathy into three distinct types: affective, somatic, and cognitive.

1) **Affective Empathy** – the ability to respond to other people's emotions appropriately.
2) **Somatic Empathy** – the ability to feel what another person is feeling.
3) **Cognitive Empathy** – the ability to understand someone's response to a situation.

Responding with empathy in these primary ways is a game changer in today's social and workplace climates, which demand a greater focus on mental health, diversity, inclusion, and engagement. For those who are more business-minded, the most compelling case for empathy rests in the bottom-line metrics. Various studies reveal that when people lead with empathy, they notice a marked increase in employee engagement, innovation, and retention. Those being led also report better feelings of mental wellness and work-life balance.

A 2021 *Forbes* article by Tracy Brower, PhD, cites new research that demonstrates empathy's importance in these areas, which led to her opining that, "Great leadership requires a fine mix of all kinds of skills to create the conditions for engagement, happiness, and performance, and empathy tops the list of what leaders must get right."[1]

Brower also cites research from the University of Virginia that discovered "when people saw their friends experiencing threats, they experienced activity in the same part of their brain which was affected when they were personally threatened. People felt for their friends and teammates as deeply as they felt for themselves."[2]

While empathy is deep rooted in some more than others, it is an undeniable human capacity. Research has also validated that the sharing of empathetic feelings breeds even more empathy. I'd like to appeal to that inborn or innate empathy right now through one of the channels I am more commonly known for—storytelling.

I GOT IT!

For more than a decade, I've shared with audiences of all sizes a particular story that changed my thoughts and theory of what great leadership looks like. In fact, this story is the foundation of the empathic leadership principles I share with experienced and emerging leaders worldwide. This

---

[1] Brower, Tracy. "Empathy Is the Most Important Leadership Skill According to Research." Forbes Magazine, 12 Sept. 2021, www.forbes.com/sites/tracybrower/2021/09/19/empathy-is-the-most-important-leadership-skill-according-to-research/?sh=7d9ae2313dc5.

[2] Brower, Tracy. "Empathy Is the Most Important Leadership Skill According to Research." Forbes Magazine, 12 Sept. 2021, www.forbes.com/sites/tracybrower/2021/09/19/empathy-is-the-most-important-leadership-skill-according-to-research/?sh=7d9ae2313dc5.

story is also the impetus for the writing of this book. It's a story I first penned in *Now I See — A Journey of Prophecy, Pain, and Purpose.*[3]

The journey began during March Madness in 2007. My mother died suddenly from a heart attack, and my grief was overwhelming. Feeling deeply melancholy one day in April of that year, I didn't have the energy to go into a big supermarket full of people to get my groceries. Instead, I opted to try a small corner grocery just outside the Indiana University college campus where I was working as an Assistant Women's Basketball Coach. My friend, John, and my son, Drew, accompanied me. We planned to make it a quick trip—to pick up a few items and then return to the house so we could finish packing for my upcoming move to Jacksonville, FL. After my mother's sudden passing, I needed to relocate to Florida to take care of my father.

I was at the grocery check-out counter when I heard the words, "I GOT IT!" ring out from the front entrance of the store like a fire alarm. The person's voice was loud and startling, like someone calling for help in a horror movie! Everyone within earshot froze in fear or confusion of what might happen next. The young man who abruptly screamed those words was now sprinting towards me! I quickly turned my head, and as I took him in full gaze, he once again yelled at the top of his lungs, "I GOT IT!"

Drew had been playing at the claw machine game at the front of the store with John. I immediately looked towards them to be sure Drew was out of danger's way. I watched John move in my direction for defensive protection. Meanwhile, every eye in the store's check-out area was wide-eyed and fixated on the screaming young man dashing towards me! I felt a wave of heat rush through my chest and a tightening of my jaw as my eyes widened in fear and disbelief.

The young man approached me and came to a clumsy halt. Then, with his left forearm against my right, he pushed me away from my cart. In that moment, my gaze was fixed on my purse, which was in the small basket area by the handlebar. Now, I grew up in Prince George's County, Maryland. Where I'm from, when a screaming stranger runs up to you and

---

[3] Jones, Vera. Now I See: A Journey of Prophecy, Pain, and Purpose. Outskirts Press, 2019.

pushes you away from your pocketbook, it's time to get ready for your close-up on the nightly news! With eyebrows furrowed, jaw tight, heart racing, fists clinched, and an arsenal of expletives geared up and ready for an oral missile launch, my instinctive fight or flight screamed, "Fight!" I deemed my Christian values and goodwill towards all people were forgivably null and void at this moment!

Face to face we stood, and again, the words "I GOT IT!" bellowed from deep inside this strange man's throat. But instead of screaming back at him or doing my best Karate Kid impression, I stood in frozen silence, because this time his exclamation was followed by his slurred speech. It sounded like, "Rickeee-poosh-da carts!" I squinted and stared deeply into his face, and I felt my heart instantly cool and soften. I felt the adrenaline leave my body, and a sense of peace and humbleness washed over me. At that moment, I noticed that not only did he slur his speech, but he also had atypical facial features. His soft eyes drooped behind his thick-framed glasses. His mouth slightly hung open, suggesting a smile that hadn't quite figured out how to form, but had a lot of pure potential. Thankfully, I was wise enough to understand, even in duress, that this young man had a cognitive disability. In an instant, my empathic light bulb clicked on with so many heartwarming revelations.

This beautiful young man wasn't trying to steal my purse or cause anyone bodily harm in broad daylight in front of a host of startled and bewildered onlookers. He was trying desperately, committedly, and enthusiastically to *help* me! He was passionately, proudly, and powerfully taking ownership of the job he had been asked to do. He was saying, in the best way he knew how, "No, Lady, in this store, it is my duty and my honor to push the carts. I cannot allow you to do it, for this is my job, my gift, my pleasure, my passion, and it is my purpose!"

"I GOT IT!"

Those three simple but powerful words changed everything for me.

(Confession: I've been telling this story for many years, and the truth is that I really don't know what this young man's name was. His speech was slurred, and this was the best interpretation I could come up with in such an awkward and tense moment. Alas, his name has lived on in legacy as "Ricky" to me and everyone I tell this story to. "Ricky, push the carts!" And that he did in a way I will never forget!)

Ricky swung my cart into the exit aisle (with my purse still in it!) and off he went, full steam ahead, out of the store. Drew and John looked at me to make sure I was okay while simultaneously trying not to laugh at the entire awkwardness of the situation or the look of complete bewilderment on my face. I followed my purse out the store, making sure to stay completely out of Ricky's way. "Let the man do his job," I always say!

We reached the car, and I opened the trunk. I placed a few bags in the trunk, checking first with Ricky to ensure it was all right for me to do so. I didn't want to find out the hard or painful way that "Ricky packs the trunk, too!" When the cart was empty, Ricky looked at me and said, "I GOT IT!" as if reassuring me it was his pleasure to help. Off he went pushing the empty cart back towards the grocery store. After he entered the store, I saw him through the big glass window and watched him run towards the checkout line. I then heard his loud "I GOT IT!" bellowing out the open door, startling the daylights out of the next unsuspecting customer. "Go, Ricky, go!" I instantly became his number one fan!

For the remaining weeks I was in Bloomington, Indiana, I could not get Ricky and "I GOT IT" out of my head. In those moments when I was down, or when I woke up less than optimistic, I would look into the mirror, yell "I GOT IT!" and smile. It was hard not to smile and admire his tenacity of purpose every time I thought of him. I even went back to shop at that grocery store a few times just to see if he was there. It was easy to know when he was. I'd hear "I GOT IT!" off in the distance when I was parking my car. I couldn't wait to see the customers' reactions. Ricky inspired me. He made me feel good about being alive, even as I grieved my mother who no longer was.

In the weeks that followed my grocery store encounter, something much more significant about Ricky's story and example of worker enthusiasm came to my consciousness. In fact, I learned many personal perspectives vicariously via Ricky that stuck with me, including lessons of empowerment, engagement, resilience, and service. I wanted that kind of contagious energy and enthusiasm in my own work ethic. I wanted to embrace the mindset that despite the fouls I may face in my life, focusing on my gifts to be significant through service would be my work and life template. "I GOT IT" would be my new mantra forevermore.

Yet, the most profound lesson I learned was the power of empathic leadership. I imagined what it must have taken to empower and engage someone like Ricky to make such a memorable impact on others. My vision of leadership changed completely. I realized that empathy was the driving force behind truly connecting with people—all people—and inspiring, motivating, and guiding them towards significance and purpose.

Ricky's boss granted him a chance to matter, to make a difference, and to take pride in his efforts to serve others. That leader cared enough to create the opportunity and the structure for Ricky to thrive. He or she helped Ricky use his strengths and showed him how he specifically fit into the bigger picture of the defined team win. Ricky was the energy, enthusiasm, and efficiency reflection of what a leader with tremendous empathy could ignite in a person.

I imagined the degree of research and active listening the manager engaged in to understand how to guide, motivate, and empower Ricky. The leader had to consider not only the tasks that needed to be done, but also the specific ways Ricky could effectively do them. To build trust with Ricky, this leader needed to make genuine connection and truly care about Ricky's perspectives, needs, orientation, and motivations. Over the years, this vicarious or imagined leadership example became very real and tangible to me. And once I became a mother of a child labeled "special needs," this leadership example resonated with me intimately.

Empathy Hits Home

At the age of 12, my son, Drew, was diagnosed with a brain tumor, called a craniopharyngioma. It was a large, life-threatening tumor that was pressing on his pituitary gland and optic nerve. He underwent emergency surgery to save his life, but it was predetermined that even what would be considered a successful surgery would leave my son faced with a difficult and challenging life, navigating through a blind or visually impaired and "differently abled" world.

As a single mother, I had learned a ton of leadership lessons the hard way, through countless trials and errors, as almost every parent can relate. None, however, came so painfully as this dark era of my child's life that was compounded with blindness, obesity, hormonal related medical emergencies and conditions, and a hearing impairment. Beyond the physical trauma, I was ill-prepared for the subsequent psychological and emotional damage that would arise from Drew being constantly teased and bullied at school. My entire soul ached as I tried to understand and lead him through his battle with depression, anxiety, and suicidal thoughts. I tell people I know so much about empathy because I have deeply lived it. I'm a witness to its power.

There were many days when the deep compassion I felt for my son drove me to search any and everywhere for solutions. While I could not know the depths of his physical or emotional pain, I could demonstrate how much I cared. I constantly communicated to him the ways in which he mattered. I became more provisionally sensitive to what he needed to feel secure and confident. I learned many things that blind and visually impaired people require to navigate and cope in a sighted world. I accepted that every day would be far from perfect during his recovery, but I made sure to celebrate even the small steps of progress. I also learned that on many days, just being there, showing how much I loved him and cared, was the only solution that mattered.

The greatest "aha" moment of the power of empathy and perspective taking came during a visit to the Helen Keller School at the Alabama Institute for the Deaf and Blind. I attended a weekend Parents Workshop for visually impaired and blind students. In one session they set up a navigation simulation where each parent had to wear goggles or blinders that simulated the perception of their child. My son, Drew, is totally blind in his right eye and has no peripheral vision in his left. So, his only sight is through a small nickel-sized hole near the left side of his nose. Therefore, I was given goggles with all parts blackened except for a small visual field. My task was to walk to a location across the campus using my son's cane. The competitor in me was determined to make it to the finish line successfully. But I walked in complete anxiety and nervousness. I bumped into things. I walked slowly, and even with encouragement from others, I felt extremely insecure. I was literally placed into my child's perceptive shoes. For those brief moments, I not only saw what he saw, but I also deeply felt what he had been feeling. My empathy grew exponentially that day, and so did my ability to lead him in a far more compassionate and productive way.

While you may be thinking that the deep-rooted empathy I experienced was due to a loving maternal bond not shared with co-workers and teammates, I hope you can still relate to how powerful empathy truly is. The main point to embrace is that the more committed you are to care, the more innovative and diverse alternatives you will seek to resolve problems, thus increasing your problem-solving effectiveness. As the leader, you too will come with your own personal problems. Even when managing your own life fouls, you will still be expected to help others manage theirs. This skillset that closely parallels parenting requires the ability to balance empathy with a responsible degree of self-care. So, my quick public service announcement to leaders is to please prioritize mental wellness and taking good care of yourself!

Realize, too, that when people come to work, their life problems come with them. They also create and encounter brand new problems with others on the job. Your team will often look to you—their leader—to help them overcome their conflicts and concerns. To be blunt, that's one of the reasons why you were chosen to be the leader. You are expected to have problem solving abilities. It's written into most leadership job descriptions. You may have thought that meant process or technical problems when you read it, but in the fine print, it meant dealing with people problems. And that includes all the confusing emotions and icky stuff like tears, frustration, sadness, anger, and defeat. Yep. All of them. Being charged to deal with these problems can often feel overwhelmingly intimidating.

Before you prematurely turn in your resignation, please understand you do not have to solve every problem. After all, you are a leader, not a magician. The good news is that the key strategy you need to apply is empathy—to care sincerely enough about others and to effectively demonstrate your desire to help them find solutions. You'll quickly discover that there is a seemingly magical element in demonstrating empathy that helps problems disappear! In fact, sometimes your magical skillset in leadership is just listening. Did you hear me? (Pun intended.) Just listen, actively and empathically. People often feel better after they have an opportunity to sound out their problems. It's called catharsis. Sometimes people don't need a solution as much as they need a caring sounding board.

Wrapping it Up

Take it from a mother, mentor, and coach who spends every day listening with compassion and concern: there is power and healing in just knowing someone truly cares. Please never underestimate this power. On many days it will prove to be your greatest leadership tool, especially when specific solutions escape you at a given moment. I've coached many leaders who feel frustrated when they have to "babysit" people problems. "I can't stand all the emotions and whining," one told me. Recognizably, leadership is challenging in this regard. Still, most leaders learn the hard way that these problems do not simply disappear by avoiding them, or by complaining how much you hate dealing with them. Rather, when they engage in a great deal of perspective-taking powered by empathy, they can create effective solutions to move people beyond their problems to progress and productivity. I can't say it enough, *"They won't care how much you know until they know how much you care."*

This is why the affiliate leadership style is one of the most crucial to develop. While progress and productivity are the desired end game, ultimately, it is the people performing the tasks to attain progress and productivity that you must prioritize. People come first. You must know your people are okay, and you sometimes must help them overcome their adversity by reminding them of the ways they can scream, "I GOT IT!" In fact, your primary leadership goal must be to develop talent by building trusted, empathic relationships, so that when these inevitable people problems arise, you are the one they trust to help them move forward.

In an ideal leadership mindset, it works like this: You know how to respond to your people appropriately *(affective empathy)*; you put yourself in their shoes to feel what they are feeling *(somatic empathy);* you understand why they may have responded the way they did to a particular situation *(cognitive empathy);* and you care about your people enough to guide them to the "I GOT IT!" mindset. You have motivational credibility with them, and it comes from the foundation of your genuine empathy.

Daniel Goleman offered the world this critical leadership nugget:

"Great leaders move us. They ignite our passion and inspire the best in us. When we try to explain why they are so effective, we speak of strategy, vision, or powerful ideas. But the reality is much more primal: Great leadership works through the emotions. No matter what leaders set out to do—whether it's creating strategy or mobilizing teams to action—their success depends on how they do it. Even if they get everything else just right, if leaders fail in this primal task of driving emotions in the right direction, nothing they do will work as well as it could or should."[4]

I learned so many leadership lessons in the years I was helping my young son overcome a brain tumor and blindness. In many ways, he is my greatest leadership success story. Since then, I've shared his story (and Ricky's) with millions of people during my years as a motivational speaker—so much so that the themes of "Trust Your Vision" and "Play Through the Foul" have become my legacy on stage. And while I always credit God for giving me the capacity for empathy, I also want to take this space to credit Ricky's leaders for showing me the true potential empathy can have on a person. I believe that fateful encounter that day in the small grocery store on the edge of the Indiana University campus was set up as a reminder to me that you do not need to have all the answers in the face of adversity. You just have to care enough about people to not give up and to seek the answers they need to be their best, especially on those days where "best" feels elusive. Empathy is like the leadership air your followers breathe. You may not recognize how much it matters until they are deprived of it. And trust me, when they are deprived, you will definitely know!

---

[4] Goleman, Daniel, et al. Primal Leadership: Learning to Lead with Emotional Intelligence. Harvard Business Review Press, 2004.

Empathy AAA Exercises

Awareness

- What CONNECTION are you making with your team members to make each of them yell "I GOT IT" in words and actions?
- List three to five things each person NEEDS to do their best work.
- What observations have led to you knowing this is what they need?

Accountability

- List the ways you desire to become more empathic. Is it to be a better listener? To do a better job of reaching out and asking people how they are feeling? Spending more time reading novels? (This can help you become more emotionally intelligent.)
- How will you be accountable to this growth area?

Action

- This week, find five opportunities to have deeper conversations with coworkers. Explore a topic or subject (within boundaries) that you may not have ever addressed before to engage how they truthfully feel. Perhaps a conversation that gives feedback on your leadership is in order.
- Find the courage to listen and be grateful for the knowledge without judgment or offense.
- Remember, seek to be IMPROVED, not approved.

CHAPTER 3

THE BIRTH OF LEADERSHIP 6-S

> *"People don't care how much you know until they know how much you care."*
> *—Theodore Roosevelt*

My father often emphasized that the most challenging question for many individuals is, "What do you want?" Intrigued by his theory, I have consistently adopted this question as a key metric for assessing the foundations for empathic leadership. Understanding what people want and need from their leaders is pivotal to leading with empathy.

To put dear old dad's theory to the test, I invite you to participate in a quick poll. When contemplating your current or prospective workplace, please rank the following factors from 1 to 6, with 1 being the most crucial and 6 the least. Consider what contributes most to your sense of engagement at work.

If you find it difficult, rephrase the questions as follows: "I can navigate various challenges at work, but **without consistent access to THIS**, my motivation to stay might be short-lived."

A) _____ Having an opportunity to use my skills and talents to do meaningful work; knowing I matter and am an important part of the team and contribute to our success.

B) _____ Trusting that I am comfortable, playing on a stable team, in a safe environment with financial rewards or benefits, and no indication of threat to them, my position, reputation, or other valued provisions.

C) _____ Knowing my leadership and/or team provides reliable guidance; stimulates innovation; works logically and smart; I have opportunities to take action, strategize, and engage in an efficient, problem-solving manner.

D) _____ Working sensibly with a clear vision, mission, guidelines, fairness, rules, and regulations; having logistical, organized processes for being productive and accountable for winning.

E) _____ Knowing my organization is fair, lives up to its promises to employees (team) and customers, and prioritizes integrity; working in a genuine culture of family honesty and openness, where I am trusted and respected.

F) _____ Believing I work in a helpful, diverse, team environment, where everyone feels valued and that being included, committed to serving, and winning together is more important than individual credit and rewards.

Was my father correct? Did you find it difficult to rank what was most important to you? Most people say that all the factors are relatively important to some degree, and they easily find something that resonates in each area. Ranking what you want or need *the most* is challenging because doing so requires concentrated evaluation and introspection.

Most people think they know what they want or need because they believe they are self-aware. In fact, research shows that 95% of people believe they are self-aware, but only 10-15% actually are.[5] My philosophy is that when people are compelled to prioritize what holds the utmost

---

[5] Kauflin, Jeff. "Only 15% of People Are Self-Aware -- Here's How to Change." Forbes Magazine, 29 June 2017, www.forbes.com/sites/jef-fkauflin/2017/05/10/only-15-of-people-are-self-aware-heres-how-to-change/?sh=1d4e48df2b8c.

importance for them, they get a genuine opportunity to deep dive into the self-awareness of what emotionally drives or motivates them the greatest.

The Leadership 6-S Assessment Key

If you placed a 1 by:

- A – you are most strongly motivated by **SIGNIFICANCE.**
- B – you are most strongly motivated by **SECURITY.**
- C – you are most strongly motivated by **SOLUTIONS.**
- D – you are most strongly motivated by **STRUCTURE.**
- E – you are most strongly motivated by **SINCERITY.**
- F – you are most strongly motivated by **SELFLESSNESS.**

I created this simple assessment not only to help people evaluate what is important to them in the workplace, but also to help leaders understand what motivated people to do the work that needed to be done. I call these **<u>S-Motivators.</u>** The beauty of this is that you do not have to administer a time-consuming 50-question survey; you can simply have a conversation with your staff or team members and have them rank their preference, just as you did.

Most organizations survey their staff to see how leadership, projects, processes, products, services, and other resources are measuring up. For leaders, however, knowing how they measure up based on a survey of generalities is not useful for their professional development. Empathic leaders need to know how they measure up in the specific areas that motivate people emotionally to perform their best. That's why a leadership survey with 50 questions and measurements can make leaders feel like they must jump through multiple hoops to succeed.

In 2013, I took a chance to answer my father's famous question, "What do you want?" I decided that I wanted a simple way to help leaders, especially young or emerging leaders, to understand what was most important for engaging and developing their people. I knew they needed one simple question to focus on. That question became the one you just answered. *"What is most important for you to feel engaged at work?"* The answer to that question reveals how to empathically lead the person who answered, because what is really being assessed is a desire based on motivation, orientation, and needs. What your followers want and need from you most is what I sum up as Leadership 6-S.

As I mentioned in the book's Introduction, when you say 6 and S together, it sounds a lot like Success! (Please don't hate me because I'm clever.) Your *leadership success* is paramount for you and your team! Over the past decade, I've spent a lot of time researching, polling, surveying, coaching, training, and simply listening to what people in various industries said they wanted and needed from their leaders. I reveal the breakdown of those poll numbers at the end of this chapter.

My research has uncovered that people want leaders who demonstrate that they care about their team and engage others accordingly in six critical areas:

1. **SIGNIFICANCE**
2. **SECURITY**
3. **SOLUTIONS**
4. **STRUCTURE**
5. **SINCERITY**
6. **SELFLESSNESS**

I discovered that most people believe all six areas are important; however, their first and second choices translate as deep motivators, or conversely as relative "dealbreakers," for engagement. In other words, when leaders fail to pay consistent attention to these fundamental elements, employee disengagement and eventual attrition was highly likely. And long before I began investigating these needs in others, I was experiencing them for myself during my painful nine months under the thumb of Coach Killjoy.

Learning from Lack

By 2012 I had been speaking, training, and consulting for about three years. Thanks to my Ricky encounter, and almost three decades of working in diverse industry spaces from corporate to academic, I thought I knew a lot about leadership. However, I realized that I was lacking in one key piece of information: what it was like to be on the front line, allowing myself to be led and developed. It was one thing to coach others from a leadership perspective. It was quite another to adopt the employee perspective and empathically feel what those being led commonly experience.

To fill this gap (and to give myself some professional stability while caring for my disabled son), I took a position as an assistant basketball coach at an NCAA Division I university. Very soon after, I was certain that accepting the position was by far the biggest mistake I had ever made in my life. In hindsight, though, I understand the divine intervention for which I was set up to live and learn: what leadership was NOT and why followers craved empathy from their leaders.

My first interview encounter with my leader, who has lived on in infamy and storytelling as "Coach Killjoy," was a good one. She was industry intelligent, articulate, experienced, and committed to winning. She was specifically looking for a "strong black woman" whose people skills, particularly relating with the players (we had a predominantly African American team), balanced her more introverted style. I clearly expressed to her that my greatest concern was returning to the busy work life of collegiate coaching as a single mother with a disabled son.

While I did not have any reservations about my capabilities to coach (that had always been a passion for me), I knew I needed a family atmosphere to succeed. I specifically wanted a place where both my son and I felt accepted—a place where people understood that one of my biggest challenges was maintaining life balance as it pertained to being present for my son, especially in unexpected moments of crisis. Although I inherently identify with a SIGNIFICANCE S-Motivator, I was also strongly motivated by SINCERITY and SECURITY at the time. I accepted the position primarily because Coach Killjoy, a young mother herself, went to great lengths to convince me she was an empathic leader with family as one of her guiding core values.

Only a couple of months into my position, I realized I had been bamboozled! Coach Killjoy was any and everything *BUT* empathic. At times her student athletes questioned if she had any compassionate emotions at all! In fairness, all good coaches are accused at times of being tough or unfair. But for Coach Killjoy, these comments hit harder because her more introverted style, coupled with her strange, sadistic vibe, often made her feel unapproachable. This was a huge reason why players flocked into my office to cry or vent. It didn't help that Coach Killjoy often told them, "I couldn't care less about your feelings!" Players complained that she was cold, distant, insensitive, and uncaring. What was odd to me was that Coach Killjoy seemed to revel in that character assessment. "I want them to fear and hate me! That's how I know I have their respect!" she would say.

When the athletic trainer reported a medical issue or concern with one of our players, Coach Killjoy asserted that the player was faking an injury or illness to get out of practice. It didn't matter if the player was diagnosed with a concussion, the flu, or a broken bone, Coach Killjoy presumed the player was pathetically weak or manipulatively conniving. When the student-athlete was finally cleared to return to practice, Coach Killjoy joked with our staff about how severely she planned to punish the player so they'd think twice about ever feigning sickness or injury again.

In another painfully memorable example, our star player was very close to her grandfather. One afternoon she received the news that he had unexpectedly passed away. That night, she played poorly. Coach Killjoy wasted no words, lashed out at her poor performance in the locker room, which brought the player to tears in front of everyone. As much as I hated it, I had to bite my tongue and couldn't jump in to defend our player. Anger, frustration, hate, and fear were all over the faces of the other players. One upset player showed up in my office soon afterwards to ask me why Coach Killjoy always acted so coldly, like she hated them. She wanted to quit and she shared that others on the team shared her fears and concerns.

In our staff meeting the next day, I made the comment that our loss wasn't just the one player's fault, and that we should consider the other variables that contributed to our demise. I added that receiving the news about her grandfather's death probably played a role in the player's mental state. Coach Killjoy barked out, "Too bad! Everyone has problems. Everyone dies. That doesn't excuse her for playing poorly!" Just when I thought I had heard it all, she added, "She's supposedly so religious. Why couldn't she just pray about it and move on?" She then snickered, as if she was proud of her ability not to care, and her ability to leave me speechless, which admittedly is a very hard thing to do.

Coach Killjoy seldom extended the benefit of the doubt to anyone. For some psychological reason, she was unable to cultivate or operate in a culture of mutual respect and trust. It didn't take long for her to turn her cynicism, lack of trust, and lack of empathy towards me. When I had to pick my son up from school or tend to a medical issue, she sarcastically quipped to my coaching colleagues that I was trying to get out of my responsibilities at work. I greatly struggled with this treatment because I was prideful, with a strong work ethic, and did not want to be thought of "less-than" because I was a single parent or because I had a disabled son. Yet that was exactly how I felt daily, and it quickly took its toll on me emotionally and motivationally.

Gasping for Leadership Air

As the weeks went by, I felt more and more perplexed as to what atrocities this style of leadership would bring next. Just when I thought it couldn't get any worse, I learned that Coach Killjoy asked one of the players to spy on the others. She wanted a full report on what was said in the locker room, especially any negative comments about her. What truly complicated matters was that the spy was one of only two white players on the team. Once the team learned about this stunt, a racial rift ensued. Instead of focusing on developmental goals and winning basketball games, players and staff now had to focus on navigating a minefield of team distrust and questions of racial inequities. Since Coach Killjoy was a bi-racial woman, I thought she would have been sensitive to the empathy needed to fully embrace diversity rather than create the tensions that would ultimately cause division.

I struggled to follow Killjoy's lead, to the point that at times I would feel utter rage. Perhaps that was the degree of emotion required for me to stop to learn the lessons. For everything vicariously vibrant my image of Ricky's leadership stirred up in me, Coach Killjoy's leadership crushed it. Instead of publicly yelling "I GOT IT," I found myself privately yelling expletives! I had never been so miserable at work, and I had never been surrounded by so many other people who were miserable too. Where was the unity? Where was the sense of family? Where was the trust? I had never felt so disengaged and disappointed in any position I had ever held.

I suddenly felt like I was walking on eggshells, gasping for air, and battling depression. My leader was not recognizing so many needs—not just from me, but from everyone. Upon examining Coach Killjoy's character, communication, and choices, I finally accepted that we did not share the same values or leadership philosophies. As an assistant coach, I knew it was my job to buy in to her leadership vision, structure, and style. Not knowing how I could make that happen or how to make things better between us kept me awake most nights. I did not want to follow this leader, and I struggled with the constant contemplation over whether I would quit or get fired. I lost countless hours obsessing over why it was all happening in the first place. I felt guilty that I wasn't being a great leader for our players because I was too upset over the lack of leadership I was receiving. I was a walking ball of confusion, anxiety, and negativity.

From Chaos to Conception

They say adversity is our greatest teacher. This certainly proved to be true for me. In Ricky's case I learned how the positive effects of empathy could be contagious; in this new scenario, I realized the negative effects from lack of empathy were just as real. I did not want to fall victim to the negativity any longer. I began journaling my experiences so I could cope and not allow my nine months of fear, fouls, and failure with Coach Killjoy to be in vain.

As I journaled, I imagined what Coach Killjoy must have experienced to have fallen so short of her responsibilities as a leader. I knew there had to be important lessons I could take away from the nightmare I was living. I realized that Coach Killjoy was a young leader who had never held a college head coaching position before and had never wrestled with such immeasurable demands. She often talked about how her most previous employer, the person she relied upon to develop her as a head coach, never empathically connected with her, and the words she used to describe their working relationship were, "I hated her." So, I surmised that Coach Killjoy was insecure and struggled with imposter syndrome on a lot of levels, passing down a boatload of negative communication and behavioral choices she learned from her leader. A few years removed from my most troubled working environment, when I reflected on these experiences, instead of feeling rage, I began to feel—you guessed it—*empathy*.

Ultimately, it was the discoveries that unfolded from both my best- and worst-case scenarios of leadership that helped me to conceive the complete picture of what was needed most for empathic leadership. I believe it took a little pain and a lot of empathy to ignite my passion to help leaders understand what their followers needed and wanted most. I took one for the team, so to speak, and I'm better for it. Now I need you to be!

Beware of Imposter Syndrome

Coach Killjoy struggled with imposter syndrome. Perhaps you do too. **Imposter syndrome** is the feeling that no matter how much you have achieved or how much you know about a particular subject matter, you feel fake, phony, inadequate, or incompetent, and you fear you will be exposed as such. When you are new to leadership and managing or directing others, this feeling can be overwhelming, particularly if you identify with perfectionism. Imposter syndrome begins as doubt and can grow into full-blown anxiety and internalized fear.

In Coach Killjoy's case, her passive aggressive behaviors, standoffishness, mean spiritedness, blaming, and bullying were protection mechanisms for her insecurities. As a first-year head coach, with little empathic mentoring, she most likely wanted to be a great coach, but she probably believed she was in over her head. I may not have recognized it while I was enduring it, but I now know imposter syndrome can show up in destructive ways I refer to as **stank face leadership.** The following symptoms are all reflective of imposter syndrome:

Confusion	Jealousy	Gossiping
Blaming	Anger	Anxiety
Belittling	Undermining	Seclusion
Secrecy	Retaliating	Passive Aggressiveness
Frustration	Self-protection	Projection

I witnessed all these knee-jerk conflict responses in my time with Coach Killjoy, but I doubt she witnessed them in herself, which is why I stress self-awareness as the cornerstone of empathic leadership development. To be clear, I'm not excusing her behaviors. I am simply applying cognitive empathy in an attempt to stand in her shoes and learn the hard-knock lessons. Her lack of compassion, passive aggressiveness, and mean-spirited conduct left both her players and staff in dysfunction and dismay, and destroyed her own opportunities for success.

Coach Killjoy's final season of a five-year tenure made the history books in the most undesirable ways for a coach. Her accomplishments included the longest losing streak, the lowest win percentage, the most losses, and the highest turnover in the program's history. Of course, statistics are only a suggestive overview of the harsh realities that truly went on behind the scenes in Coach Killjoy's program. The losses off the court were far greater than those on it. Many players either quit or transferred, and the program experienced tremendous staff turnover. And her reputation preceded her, as the university had a difficult time recruiting new players. In an age of rampant social media, bad news and bad behavior traveled fast.

Most poignant to consider is that Coach Killjoy had a solid knowledge of basketball and was a solid tactician of the sport. So she wasn't a poor leader due to lack of technical knowledge. Rather, her greatest downfall was a tremendous lack of empathy. We see this occur in the corporate world too, where many leaders gain favorable promotion because they have admirably competent skillsets. But empathic leadership is a mindset first, then a skillset. Too many organizations fail to recruit or prepare leaders to excel in this area, making it one of the greatest downfalls of leadership. It's especially evident in sports, where the value of "being tough" is easily and often misdirected.

I've shared Coach Killjoy's story because sometimes it's easier to visualize the kind of leader you don't want to be. Seeing the negative can help bring the positive image of what you do want into better focus. Most people believe they would never be harsh or cruel or passive aggressive. However, the pressures that come with leadership can catch people off guard and under-prepared for how to respond, leaving many leaders with destructive fight or flight responses to conflict.

Learning to lead from a position of empathy helps to alleviate the negative reflexes of imposter syndrome, because you learn how and where to build the individual trust necessary to ask perspective-taking questions. As you engage your vulnerability as curiosity, it becomes a strength rather than a weakness. With time and practice, you learn the importance of expressing your concerns directly to those you are leading or working with and listening empathically for their concerns. You do this because **you seek to be _improved_ to help them, rather than _approved_ to be judged by them**. That is the empathic leadership difference—building trust and connections, not conflict and chaos.

We All Want 6-S

Have you ever experienced a time where one person made a single comment that stuck with you? I had that moment when our star player, who had just gotten a tongue-lashing from Coach Killjoy in front of the whole team for her lack of leadership and production, asked a simple question. With tears in her eyes, in her typically soft and humble voice, she uttered my "aha moment" question: _"If I'm NOT a good leader, then who is teaching me how to be?"_ You could have heard a pin drop in that locker room! It was a profound question and a dagger to my heart. As much as I wanted to say, "Yeah, Killjoy! Answer that!" I realized I was part of Coach Killjoy's staff. I, too, was accountable as a failed teacher and leader.

Often, it is easy for us to point the finger at what someone else did wrong. It is harder for us to empathically step into their leadership shoes and identify what we would have done affectively or cognitively differently in the same scenario. This is where the true developmental lessons lie. While you can learn much from examples of the leader you want to be, I assert that envisioning the leader you _DO NOT_ want to be can keep you humble and mindful of the importance of empathy in leadership. The lack of empathic action in leadership often causes painful, unwanted circumstances and outcomes. Since most people pay more attention to pain, a negative situation can have a greater impetus for implementing change. I always say, _**"We don't grow in places of comfort. We grow when we are uncomfortably challenged to change."**_

I invite you to contrast elements of Coach Killjoy's reign to that of the "I GOT IT" leadership legacy. I've purposely created for you vivid pictures of a tale of two leaders, and I encourage you to take an honest look into how your own character values, communication, and choices reflect or could reflect either example in the various scenarios.

Begin by asking yourself these questions:

1. "What happens if I *DON'T* lead with empathy?"
2. "What should I focus on to ensure that I do lead with empathy?"
3. "How can I help the people I lead, even in the face of adversity, demonstrate an 'I GOT IT' mindset?"

Envision your answers with clarity. Really see them. Then, deeply feel the impact. You'll soon discover the case for empathy can be best wrapped up as this: *"Empathy inspires a leader's wit and wisdom; lack thereof invites a leader's contempt and confusion."*

You got it?

Here's what else I hope you get. No one goes into leadership *wanting* to be a bad boss or to be a jerk leader. Sometimes leaders feel like they are in over their head, especially when they are new or improperly trained. For these people, every day feels like a complete drudge with people problems rounding every corner, and the new leader feels ill-equipped to manage them all. This is when the "babysitting people who get on my nerves" feeling of frustration overwhelms the leader's desire to empathically connect. Taking care of others the way we wish to be cared for seems like such a simple concept, but this simplistic value can get pushed to the back burner as the desire and pressure to perform clouds its essentialism.

Granted, your diverse team of personalities that you oversee will need many things from you. Fortunately, I've summed them up into six simple categories that all start with the letter S. Hence, the term **Leadership 6-S**. These are the six attributes or areas of importance I suspect no one told Coach Killjoy her players needed from her most. These are the same six areas Ricky's leaders likely delivered with excellence.

These are the six areas most needed to demonstrate empathy and empower your team to success:

1. **SIGNIFICANCE** – Everyone wants to matter and will do their best work when they know specifically how they are valued and how they can best contribute. Picture people arriving at work daily with an "I GOT IT" disposition. Praise, encourage, and motivate people sincerely and regularly. **People appreciate it when you help them see how they make a difference and thank them for their contribution and service.**

2. **SECURITY** – We all need stability and safety, not just physically, but psychologically. Your positive attitude, instruction, and assurance that everything will work out, all provisions will be met, and their positions are secure offers peace of mind and builds trust. Gone are the days of the big, bad boss who threatens termination if his demands aren't met. Fear is NOT a desired motivator. *People want you to demonstrate faith and care about their safety and wellbeing.*

3. **SOLUTIONS** – Your ability to solve problems is instrumental to your leadership role. However, you don't have to do it alone. Knowing how to involve your team to build a culture of accountability is a far better choice for creating solutions. Involve others for their input as this also bolsters their intellect and self-worth. *People appreciate your knowledge and wisdom most when you are helping them grow their own problem-solving abilities.*

4. **STRUCTURE** – Creating and communicating a vision and mission as well as an organized and consistent framework of goals, rules, responsibilities, systems, regulations, and discipline is necessary for organizational as well as individual growth. *People want you to assure them they are sensibly and systematically working towards a positive purpose.*

5. **SINCERITY** – At the core of every great organization and every great leader must be an integrity of values and a commitment to honesty and fairness. Words and deeds should align, and a feeling that people are open and genuine should resonate. *People want to trust you and know they are trusted by you to do good and to be good.*

6. **SELFLESSNESS** – Never underestimate the power of inclusiveness, unity, fairness, collaboration, and the enjoyment of working with others in a family or team environment. Going above and beyond for something bigger than yourself gives people a sense of pride and purpose. *People want you to be a team player as much as you are the team leader, and to encourage their selfless commitment with your example.*

Wrapping Up

True, empathic leadership isn't babysitting; it isn't making excuses for bad behavior; it isn't coddling people's emotions; it doesn't require a PhD in psychiatry. True, empathic leadership is having the courage, compassion, and curiosity to demonstrate that you care so you can connect, inspire, and engage people towards purpose. Even when you don't agree with a person's behavior, you show empathy when you try to understand the perceptions, feelings, or beliefs behind the behavior. With that knowledge comes growth, wisdom, and opportunities for conflict resolution.

So, I ask you the big question. What do you want and need to be engaged for success? What do your people want and need? What does it look like? If you cannot envision who you want to be, start with who you don't want to be and develop your picture from there. Know what you need to create the empathic connection that will make your leadership great. Whatever that individual picture is for you, harness the six key areas to focus your empathic energy. People are looking for your character, communication, and choices to promote **SIGNIFICANCE, SECURITY, SOLUTIONS, STRUCTURE, SINCERITY, and SELFLESSNESS.** In the following chapters, we will deep dive into each of these six attributes so you can learn how to activate the power of **Leadership 6-S** for your empathic **leadership success!**

Empathy AAA Exercises

Awareness

Following are the results of the poll statistics I received over a six-year period (2017 to 2023) from a variety of industries, including government, corporate, K-12 academic, university, non-profit, and religious sectors. The Leadership 6-S Assessment was administered through group survey as well as individual polling through coaching sessions. In all, I accumulated over 1400 responses.

Results for the inquiry, **"Which of the following is MOST important for you to feel engaged at work?"**

- SIGNIFICANCE = 36%
- SECURITY = 14%
- SOLUTIONS = 9%
- STRUCTURE = 13%
- SINCERITY = 12%
- SELFLESSNESS = 16%

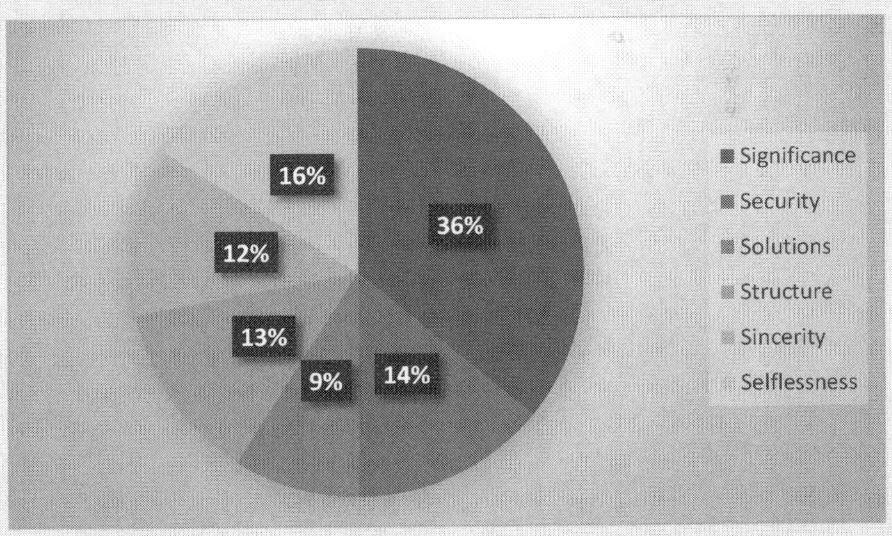

Accountability

- Now that you have an awareness of how people generally respond to the Leadership 6-S Assessment, what do you think will be the most common S-Motivator for your team?

- Set a date to test your individual team members or to conduct a group assessment.

- List two to three ways you plan to become more actively attentive for empathic growth and development.

Action

An hour of connecting may be worth a year of productivity!

- At your next meeting, give your team the Leadership 6-S Assessment survey and then discuss the results.

- Learn your team's S-Motivators and engage them to learn each other's orientation, needs, and motivations as well.

- Ask what specific ways your team desires to be led by you.

- Share your personal S-Motivator and clarify what values and communication elements are most important for the team to win, especially if conflict arises.

CHAPTER 4

SIGNIFICANCE

The canvas is complete. The image of Ricky and the words "I GOT IT" are memorialized forevermore within these pages and, with your support, within your organization—"I GOT IT!" That's it. Ricky pushes the carts! That's the visual! As a leader, your ultimate aspiration and source of joy lie in a team radiating enthusiasm, collectively exclaiming "I GOT IT" with unwavering passion for their roles and service they deliver. Perhaps they aren't audibly saying it, but the message is unmistakably conveyed through their body language and the excellence of their work. They harbor a profound belief that they are significant, making a meaningful impact, and their skills, talent, dedication, and service are valued and appreciated by customers, colleagues, leadership, and the organization overall.

I imagine Ricky enjoyed pushing the carts because they are fun to push. Employees doing work they enjoy benefits an organization's culture and bottom line. But let's not forget the motivational impetus of Ricky hearing customers say "thank you" or seeing the smiles on people's faces when he rolled the cart of groceries to their car. Let's not overlook the inherent gratitude he must have felt even if he did not have complete cognitive comprehension. For Ricky, sitting alone in a back room counting cans of corn or stocking shelves may have been okay, but I doubt it would have held comparable SIGNIFICANCE for him. Working directly with people where he could see, hear, and feel he was making a difference of service mattered most.

I, like the majority of people I have polled, am most driven and empowered by SIGNIFICANCE. Many entrepreneurial-minded types are. As such, this may prove to be the easiest chapter for me to write because I am most aligned with this motivation. When I'm speaking on stage, I enjoy it very much because it fuels my feelings of SIGNIFICANCE. Consciously choosing to do things you enjoy is a level of decision-making to which you naturally adapt soon after you mature past the age of 50. (I'll check my AARP handbook to be certain, but I'm pretty sure that's true.)

I'll be the first to admit that my favorite part of being a motivational speaker are the moments right after I get off stage, when people approach me and share how something I said resonated with them and empowered or encouraged them to improve or transform their lives. Talk about an emotional high! Wow! I love hearing their personal stories, as it helps me think of ways I can do and say even more. Those moments are worth all the preparation, pre-stage jitters, uncomfortable heels, and stage make-up. They let me know that I helped. I mattered! They make me eager to get back up there and do it all again. That is my purest motivation—to motivate others—simply knowing I make a difference.

One of the greatest pleasures I derive from coaching and training is similar. When I help walk people through their challenges, point them in the direction of progress or prosperity, and (eventually) tangibly see their development transpire, it is a life high like no other. I feel joyfully purposeful. I imagine it's similar for all the teachers, social workers, clergy, first responders, and community volunteers who aren't driven by a paycheck, who make a magnanimous, selfless commitment to serve others daily. These are likely your SIGNIFICANCE S-Motivator types. Here are some things you should know to empathically connect, resonate, and motivate them towards greatness.

If SIGNIFICANCE is YOUR S-Motivator you likely seek these things…

✓ Understanding of HOW you specifically make a difference
✓ Opportunities to regularly use your skills and gifts

✓ Work or vocation that feels meaningful or that you are passionate about
✓ Service to others or leading, guiding, coaching others
✓ Acknowledgement, praise, recognition, or appreciation for a job well done
✓ Inspiration and motivation; stimulation of the emotional through service
✓ Knowing your contribution helped progress towards the "WIN"

If you are leading people with a strong SIGNIFICANCE S-Motivator, here is what they seek from you…

✓ Respect for *how* they make a difference and how they feel about what they do
✓ Attention to what they do well and what needs improvement to be their best
✓ Recognition, which is often far more important than material rewards
✓ Sincere praise or appreciation, but some prefer it privately rather than publicly
✓ Training with consistent follow up and practical application
✓ Upward mobility opportunities for leadership or greater service
✓ Communication of how they *specifically* contribute and make a difference
✓ Realization that prolonged menial or busy work feels stagnating or even insulting

What Happens When You Don't Serve Up Significance?

You've likely seen or experienced "lack of significance" in many work-places, especially if you have a strong SIGNIFICANCE Motivator. You become bored, aloof, or easily distracted. You try to get energized about your job or your responsibilities, but you don't feel motivated or energized to do it. Once upon a time, you set goals and met challenges with excitement. You were productive and felt powerful. Now you feel pathetic and procrastinating. Office gossip wasn't a thing for you, but now it's the only thing that brings any entertainment. The complaining starts. The work stops.

The questions pour in. "What's the point of it all?" "What's my motivation?" "Does this job even matter?" "Do I even matter?" "Does my boss even care?" "Does anyone care?" "How am I making a difference and why should I stay when there are so many other possibilities out there?"

Then the answers show up, and they aren't productive ones. "I can't do that." "I won't do that." "That's not even my job." "I can't come in today…. tomorrow's not looking good either." "I quit."

If you're the leader, you may notice one of your most energetic employees, once full of potential and passion, is now leading the cancerous culture brigade. It's your job to get them back in line. But because you don't know that they are empowered by a sense of SIGNIFICANCE, you discipline, express your disappointment, and perhaps even threaten, further working against the very motivation they need to turn things around. Your lack of empathy or understanding of how much they not only want, but *need,* to matter has left you with a disengaged worker and a less-than-productive and positive culture. People who desire to make a difference typically do. But once they shut down, their contagious energy takes others with them in the opposite direction.

This type of scenario happens often because SIGNIFICANCE has proven to consistently rank the number one or number two motivator in over half of workers polled. To illustrate the power of SIGNIFICANCE, I have taken the liberty to share some case studies from my client files. The names have been creatively changed to protect the innocent (and to show you how clever I can be … after all, sarcasm is a second language for me!). As you read each scenario, consider how you might have said or done something differently to demonstrate greater empathy. Think about the needs, orientation, and motivation from the perspective of someone with a strong SIGNIFICANCE motivator who you know needs to matter.

Case Study 1
"ANITA MATTYR"

Anita was a former supervisor over a group of customer service representatives. Her boss was disappointed with the low call productivity from Anita's group. He also received a few complaints regarding poor employee engagement, gossip, and silos, so he moved Anita into what was communicated as a "lateral" move in pay but no supervisory responsibilities. Without receiving clear communication or understanding as to what she was doing wrong, or how she could improve, Anita took the move hard and considered it an embarrassing demotion.

Once one of the most knowledgeable managers the company had, Anita transformed into an unproductive gossiper and complainer. Senior management questioned what to do with her next. They called me in to diagnose and consult. It turns out Anita had a tremendously high SIGNIFICANCE motivator. Her greatest strength, passion, and need was to feel helpful leading others. When placed in a non-supervisory position, she felt lost and became disengaged from her job. *She no longer understood how she mattered,* nor did she receive constructive guidance on how she could improve. Her lack of deliverables and low morale was evident from it.

Through the lens of empathy, the senior leadership team realized that greater leadership training and better communication regarding how Anita needed to manage her team could have resulted in a different outcome. No one ever even asked her whether she enjoyed managing others, and if so, how much. Had they inquired, they would have discovered that leading others was the part of the job that kept her most engaged. In fact, she was passionate about helping others through leadership. Without it, the job was just a job, and it showed.

Case Study 2
"CARA NEMOUR"

Cara was a worker dynamo! She had pure driving energy and could work circles around the average employee. She was extremely efficient in her position, often aiding others when they asked for advice or assistance. Over the years she became a relative Mama Bear, which unfortunately translated into her being viewed as interfering, micromanaging, and self-important. She adopted a perception of, "I do all of the work around here and no one appreciates it." As a result, people labeled her as "difficult to work with" even though she was by far the most knowledgeable and productive.

When she learned how her peers and leaders felt about her being pushy and micromanaging, she stopped caring and helping. Naturally, this sudden change was apparent and had a negative impact on the team. In private coaching, Cara shared with me how she spent a decade in her position, always by far the most efficient, yet she felt unappreciated for her talents. The lack of upward mobility was unsettling, but she shared with me that she would have tolerated it if she could have gotten a "thank you" now and then. She felt that people took her talents and willingness to help for granted, and now, of all things, they thought she was a micromanager. She was defeated and she was angry.

It occurred to me that Cara's interfering and micromanaging were attention seeking tactics. She thought the more she did things herself or the more she appeared important, maybe she'd have a greater chance to be recognized and appreciated as such. She felt a lack of appreciation from the leader for so long that it became a source of deep-rooted resentment. Without recognizing it herself, she acted out in destructive ways, hoping to somehow claim the appreciation she never felt. By the time I began coaching Cara, she already made up her mind to resign and to apply for another position where she thought a new start would afford her a sense of greater recognition and appreciation. She was tired of being the top dog but feeling like the insignificant runt of litter.

Why SIGNIFICANCE is So Important

At the core of who we are, we all know we are here for a purpose. Even if we do not know the exact purpose, we sense we were created to do good things, important things, helpful things. We were created to be SIGNIFICANT. Without this sense of purpose, we feel lost and lonesome. We want the life we lead to mean something in some way to somebody. We absolutely need to matter, for why else would we consistently do for others? We know that the world would become a most selfish place if we were only here for ourselves. Some may argue that is where we are headed, even though a world where every person fends for themselves is a scary and dark reality to fathom.

This feeling of SIGNIFICANCE will always motivate us to give rather than get. But here's the irony: In giving, we do get. We get a sense of satisfaction, of accomplishment, of service. And this feeling is powerful and contagious. How do you know that you have made a difference? A very simple but sincere "thank you" is all it takes. Feeling appreciation, whether from word or deed, is empowering. Unfortunately, in today's busy and demanding workplace, the expectation of service often comes without the reciprocal of gratitude. You may be able to tolerate it for a while, but it isn't sustainable forever.

At times, leadership can feel terribly thankless. In addition to feeling a sense of purpose, leaders want to feel valued too. The good news for leaders with a high SIGNIFICANCE motivator is that you set the example. When you empathically demonstrate to your team your understanding of how much it matters to others to make a difference, your team will work harder to make a difference, therefore elevating your leadership value. In other words, you elevate your own SIGNIFICANCE every time you empower others to elevate theirs. SIGNIFICANCE is the gift that keeps on giving. Thank you for yours! Here are a couple of my favorite examples.

Case Study 3
"MARV ELLOS"

Marv is my favorite example of SIGNIFICANCE Motivation. I had the opportunity to work for him years ago and would have followed him to the moon without a rocket ship had I desired to remain in that career field. While at this company, I met Chase, a young man with no clear direction when Marv brought him on board at a Fortune 500 Mortgage Banking company. Chase's quick growth in the mortgage industry was the best reflection of Marv's empathic leadership. When Marv took a new position at a new company, Chase was the first to follow.

Chase struck me as a naturally loyal and highly intelligent man. But his loyalty wasn't to the corporation. His loyalty was to Marv. His intelligence insisted he stick with the best leader we both admitted we had ever worked for. For Chase, it was about working under Marv's empathic leadership that made the difference. Marv always empowered Chase's SIGNIFICANCE and service and knew what it took to coach him to be his best. This came with high financial reward to both Marv and Chase, as Chase was always one of the top three producers in every corporation he worked for. Growing and working together at four different mortgage corporations was high proof of the kind of loyalty and commitment empathic leadership can inspire.

In sports, we talk about coaches whose players would "run through the wall" for them. While I don't suggest you test that saying literally, I think you can embrace the metaphor figuratively. Once again, it's the "I GOT IT" mindset every great leader hopes to inspire in their followers. As a leader, you'd like to affect the kind of transformative leadership that makes people desire to give the best of what they have, perhaps what they don't even know they have, because you have empathically tapped into all the ways they can make a difference and do great things for a greater good. Few leaders actually do it to the degree of Marv Ellos, but I believe all should aspire to.

Case Study 4
"KAREN ABOCHU"

When I surveyed her team, Karen Abochu received raving reviews for her leadership. I have surveyed a lot of teams personally, and I have researched even more, but I have never seen higher regard for leadership than Karen Abochu. "Best supervisor I've ever had," the comments read. "I trust her 100%." This was uncommon praise based on my previous experience with federal government employees. When I had the chance to talk to a few of Karen's team members, I asked what made her worthy of such esteem.

They all cited her affiliative style of leadership and how she clearly made them aware of their SIGNIFICANCE to the team, constantly moving them towards growth and development opportunities. She cared about them personally, not just their work lives and performance. One worker said that she was very easy to talk to; she was a good listener and always gave great advice. Another person said, "I stay late or work on weekends sometimes because I never want to let her down. She tells me to stop working so hard all the time, but I just want to do a good job for her." Yet another added, "Karen makes you feel like family."

Having met and consulted with Karen personally, I realized she possessed genuine integrity. She had a caring, honest, and sweet personality, yet she had a seriousness about the work that needed to be done. Her conversations were always specifically about the people doing the work and what she felt each contributed to the team. She took pride in each of her employees, offering a lot of praise for their accomplishments, but she was also direct about the areas where she felt each needed to improve. She held regular check-in meetings with her team, and sometimes just talked about their families or whatever was on their minds that day. Karen Abochu epitomized leadership empathy and her superpower was helping others feel significant.

To empathically lead with SIGNIFICANCE means you must demonstrate a vested interest in each individual team member. You must connect with them on a personal level to know what makes them tick. When you discover they are driven by SIGNIFICANCE, you will realize how important it is for them to achieve through service. Therefore, assigning what they feel would be "busy work" may lead to disengagement over time, unless you are savvy enough to help them see how that busy work is making a huge difference to help someone.

Your character must ooze integrity, because to get the best out of your SIGNIFICANCE motivated team members, they must value and trust everything you say. Motivation, service, family, helping others, and achievement are additional character values that resonate. An affiliate or coaching style of leadership fare well with people driven by SIGNIFICANCE. Prioritizing people and choosing to care about what they care about is the best way to get them to go above and beyond.

When it comes to communication, simply saying "good job" is not enough. Take it further, such as, "When you did XYZ, that was exactly what we needed. This made a huge difference and was a big reason why we got the win." Be very specific as to "how" your SIGNIFICANCE person is contributing. Likewise, if they are missing the mark, be specific as to "how" they can do better and "why" it is so important to the team, customers, or to you that they do. Make no mistake, fluffy compliments won't cut it, unless you are dealing with a narcissist. This S-Motivator group of folks needs to sincerely feel they are making a difference in specific ways, and they look to you and your empathic leadership to make that happen!

Wrapping Up SIGNIFICANCE

Always remember: *you elevate your own SIGNIFICANCE every time you empower others to believe in theirs.* In other words, empowering others is contagious. The more you extend gratitude for a job well done, the more that people are likely to repeat the action. It feels good to feel appreciated. Even better, the act of extending that gratitude makes you feel significant as well. As the leader, your extension of recognition, encouragement, or empowerment carries a lot of weight.

While some people may be motivated greater than others, realize that everyone wants to matter and feel like they have contributed positively in some way. So, dive into connecting with your team one-on-one to see what makes them feel significant, whether it's pushing carts or crunching numbers to figure out a difficult problem. The answer will be different for everyone. But at its best, what will be the same is a team or organization of people who take their jobs seriously, serve passionately and committedly, and demonstrate loud and clearly, *"I GOT IT!"*

SIGNIFICANCE AAA Exercises

Awareness

One of the best ways to empower people towards SIGNIFICANCE is to spend quality time with them and engage in the conversation needed to get to know their gifts, talents, skillsets. Then, help them understand how they make a difference. Waiting until an annual evaluation moment to have a meeting can often cause duress, as it feels punitive, judgmental, and unfair, especially if you must deliver an unfavorable report. These meetings can also feel superficial, regardless of the information shared. Therefore, prioritize time to set or review goals and job duties, and to connect and build trust personally as well as professionally.

Assess the following and think about what changes you need to implement to empower SIGNIFICANCE.

- How often do you have one-on-one meetings with your staff or team?
- What understanding do you have of each person's orientation, needs, and motivations?
- Do you keep a written profile on each employee with their motivations and goals?
- How do you currently show appreciation, recognize, or reward?

Accountability

Knowing what to say to connect with your individual employees or team members is important. You are busy. You need to maximize the quality time you spend together. Here are some quality time meeting hacks:

- **Ask more than you tell!** This is how you learn!
- Occasionally try icebreakers or use assessment tools such as Communication/Social Styles to learn how to adequately "play catch" in your communication.
- Ask, "What do you enjoy most about this job?" and "What motivates you on a tough day?"
- Ask questions to discover pain points and needs.

- Get to know the personal, more vulnerable side, not just the professional. (Asking "What is something difficult you've had to overcome?" can be insightful and allows you to be empathic.)

- Be vulnerable to share your own relatable "perseverance story."

- Stress the importance of constant improvement (not approval) and the big picture goal.

- **Be specific** as to **"HOW"** a person matters to achieve the greater goal and is appreciated.

- Set clear goal metrics and follow up plans with a positive attitude and enthusiasm.

- Ask, "What can I do to motivate you or to be a great leader for you?"

- Ask, "If you were Leader for the Day, what is the first thing you'd improve?" and "What would you keep?" ("What's working, what's not?")

- When possible, share a lunch, walk, or outside activity away from the workplace to build connection.

Action

From the list above, choose two or three meeting hacks (or create your own) to implement. Set a date to meet with your individual staff or team members within the next 30 days. Start a written profile so you can maintain a visual guide of what empowers each individual towards significance.

CHAPTER 5

SECURITY

While most people do not and may never work with someone with a cognitive disability, we can all learn important lessons from Ricky's example. Imagine the deep level of perspective taking and empathy required to help Ricky feel safe, protected, and cared for at that grocery store. The store managers had to consider all the potential physical health hazards as well as psychological safety concerns of Ricky addressing strangers and pushing their carts. They had to be forward thinkers who considered whether people would try to take advantage of him, make fun of him, or even strike out at him in fear, much like I almost did before my senses caught up to my impulse.

But I suspect the leaders took it even further and even considered things like Ricky's health benefits and transportation needs. His managers likely understood Ricky required assistance getting to work. Maybe they were even empathic enough to offer him a ride home if he needed it. The grocery leaders probably knew a little about Ricky's family situation and recognized their importance to him. They knew it would not be fair or ethical to take advantage of Ricky's finances, and they likely considered how much it meant for Ricky to have a job and to feel secure, self-sufficient, and independent.

We all want to know we are secure in our places of work. We want to be assured our paychecks will arrive on time, in the right amount, if not more! (Nothing like an unexpected bonus!) We want benefits and wages that provide for our future savings, as well as the future provisions for our families. We desire a stable and safe workplace environment, including protocols for what to do if the environment becomes unsafe. We thrive with the peace of mind that we won't lose our jobs unexpectedly and that we have an opportunity for growth in our employment endeavors. We cherish those days off for vacation, sick leave, mental health, or death of a loved one. Show us a leader who cares about these things and understands how important these provisions are to our well-being and to our families, and we are most likely to show our loyalty in return.

Leaders don't often think about what makes people feel secure, because many organizations have an entire Human Resources department dedicated to these things. But when an employee desperately needs a day off because a parent or child is ill, they don't call Human Resources. They call you—their supervisor. In a single moment of need, you communicate one of two things: either "I care about your security and what you need," or "I don't care; just do your work; that's all that matters."

The leader sets the tone for how an organization empathically cares about the security of its employees. The leader should be aware that an employee has two weeks of unused vacation plus ten unused sick days, and maybe it's a good time for the employee to take a break, without feeling vulnerable. Unfortunately, we often hear about excessive, accumulated leave in organizations. Even more common are complaints from workers who are leery or overly concerned about missing time from work. You've likely witnessed various scenarios, such as when John, after the birth of his baby, comes in looking like he hasn't slept in a week. Then there's Jane, the single mother with three school-aged kids, who comes in weak and weary with flu symptoms. And don't forget about Julia, who sits behind a desk, motionless, eyes closed, head in hands, with a migraine headache. Without empathy, we reason these types are just workaholics. A deeper dive into empathy helps us realize these types have been made to feel guilty for missing time from work, or worse, fear being punished in some way because of it.

In these instances, the leader's compassion and understanding is critically important and often overlooked. While a few bad actors do try to take advantage of their paid time off, without proof of such behavior, it is better to err on the side of empathy than to suggest dishonesty and distrust. People with a strong SECURITY motivator are typically already conscientious about the importance of their work, and they usually take time off only when it is absolutely necessary. Additionally, nearly 80% of working Americans live paycheck to paycheck.[6] Thus, many workers are driven and motivated to work by their pay and benefits. Leaders who underestimate the power of SECURITY as a motivator often find themselves leading a fear-empowered culture and carrying all the heavy baggage that comes with it.

If SECURITY is your S-Motivator, you likely seek these things....

- ✓ The feeling of comfort in a stable and consistent work environment
- ✓ Financial stability and reliability
- ✓ Trusted benefits, time off when needed, and reliable resources
- ✓ Belief your job position is secure with no threat to layoff or termination
- ✓ Belief your position on the team and within the organization is valued and trusted
- ✓ Physically safe environment, workplace, and job responsibilities
- ✓ Psychologically safe environment (happy with my job and what I do)
- ✓ Respected, legitimate, growth-oriented company

---

[6] Sweeney, Erica. "Most Americans Living Paycheck to Paycheck This Year, Survey Finds." Investopedia, 18 Sept. 2023, www.investopedia.com/most-americans-report-living-paycheck-to-paycheck-new-survey-finds-7970611.

If you are leading people with a strong SECURITY S-Motivator, here is what they seek from you....

- ✓ Positive reinforcement that all is well
- ✓ Consistent behavior and attitude
- ✓ Approachability
- ✓ Understanding of their financial needs
- ✓ Concern about their health needs or needs of their families
- ✓ Clarity of rewards and benefits as well as negative consequences
- ✓ Fair treatment (Note: Be sure you have agreement on what is deemed to be "fair")
- ✓ Demonstration that they are trusted and that you can be trusted, too

What Happens When You Don't Serve Up SECURITY?

Over time, employees who feel insecure at work act out their insecurities in destructive and sometimes irreparable ways. Human beings are wired to think far more negatively than to trust naturally out of protection and self-preservation instincts. I've heard of everything from time-card fraud to once-reliable employees stealing toilet paper and supplies in their "preparing for the worst" vulnerabilities. (I've yet to figure out how toilet paper ranks so high on the self-preservation list. We witnessed this same phenomenon during COVID-19 in epic magnitude. Fear of the unknown is a strange motivator, indeed.)

You may have seen or personally experienced the kind of fear in the workplace that produces "yielding," which is when workers exhibit passive-aggressive behaviors that reflect an "I don't agree with this, but I'm not saying anything" attitude. Your employees or team members pretend to be okay, but they intentionally do the least amount of work to get by in their acquiescence. When you notice a lack of passion, performance, or productivity that once existed but now does not, and you just can't seem to logically understand why, there is a good chance your SECURITY S-Motivated team may very well be deflated or defeated.

The more obvious signs that you may not be stimulating a culture of SECURITY is when you recognize cynical remarks spoken in jest. You may hear verbal cues like the words "quit," "fired," or "lose my job" being used that you never heard before. You also may notice that uncomfortable "temperature change" when you walk in the room—a sudden chill in meetings that reflects a cold demeanor towards you or the organization. The evident body cues (whether in person or via video conference) include folded arms, sighs, eye-rolling, or slumping of shoulders or bodies in chairs. For video meetings, employees keeping their camera off when it used to be on can be a subtle indicator of negative change. Verbally you may hear defensive questions like, "You mean to tell me they want us to do all of this work on top of what we are already doing without more pay?"

Disgruntlement or even anger over lack of raises, promotions, benefits, or resources are also clear communication that insecurity exists. Complaints or grievances about workload, unfair wages, too much time commitment, unfairness, or discrimination often occur when people lack the feeling of SECURITY that would otherwise help keep them engaged and motivated at work. Eventually, silos and an "us vs. them" worker mentality will take the workplace culture hostage, making it difficult for you as the leader to manage effectively.

The more empathic communication you can apply in the form of asking specific and sincerely compassionate questions to elicit truthful answers, the better your chances for understanding your culture of SECURITY. For example, you could open a meeting by saying, "Let's take a minute to talk about the announcement of the forthcoming merger. How is everyone feeling? What concerns do you have? I know I have my own questions, but I want to hear yours."

Ultimately, when SECURITY is compromised, you experience high turnover, as well as self-protection measures like grievances, lawsuits, and negative social media. The most common habit I have identified is the "quiet quitting" that can last for years. People do the least they can in their jobs as they secretly search for another or wait for the shoe to drop. If you lack SECURITY, you may want to keep an eye on your workplace toilet paper inventory! Laugh now, but remember, many honest words are spoken in Vera's jest!

Case Study 1
"Jose F."

My consulting partner and I conducted a series of team building sessions for a small governmental department. Team morale had dropped significantly along with the critical employee satisfaction numbers. In a group setting, we encouraged individuals to talk about a general fear (spiders, snakes, heights, etc.) and one major fear or frustration they had been experiencing on the job. Jose F. was quick to emotionally announce, "Quite honestly, I am afraid of losing my job." His sentiment was then echoed by three of the other ten people in the room. (Notice the contagion).

Government is one of the few places I know of where job security is most assured. What could have possibly caused such a feeling of insecurity? All fingers pointed towards a supervisor who was condescending in tone, created a leadership "us vs. them" environment, and communicated a lack of trust in his employees. One participant needed to leave work early on a couple of occasions to pick up her kids from school when they were sick. She revealed that she felt torn between caring for her family and the potential of losing her job. Jose F. chimed in, "It's very threatening to work here. You can't even look after your own family without fear of being treated like you're a criminal. I never feel safe here."

Given the opportunity to meet and coach the supervisor, I discovered something precarious. The supervisor also lived in a state of worry and doubt. He, too, felt uncertain and unstable in his position as a supervisor. He had been thrown into a leadership role—leading the same peers he once worked alongside without proper training or concern for how difficult such a leadership task could be. On his first day as a supervisor, he learned that he would have to formally reprimand an employee. This instantly cast him into a negative light with his former peers. The leader admitted that since the beginning he was afraid of disappointing his leadership and failing his assignment. He had been projecting his own insecurities upon his staff ever since. It had proven difficult for him to give to others the empathy or SECURITY concerns he never received. Nothing spreads faster through company culture than lack of SECURITY.

Case Study 2
"Coach Yourdon"

Coach Yourdon was a driven winner. He was a high-profile, flashy kind of guy, and the thought of his reputation being damaged was unbearable. He secured a head-coaching position at a prestigious university, and he slowly began a style of coaching that grew out of his subconscious insecurities. He often said things like, "If we are not careful, these kids will get us fired," to his staff and co-workers.

People perceived Coach Yourdon as angry and unpredictable. He coached and managed from a constant place of fear, and he threatened everything from scholarships to jobs. For a short while, his style produced winning teams and reputable success. Fear can definitely be a motivator. But it wasn't sustainable. After a lengthy tenure of creating and leading an extremely toxic culture, Coach Yourdon was terminated in a nationally publicized scandal when 12 of his 15 players left the team, transferring from the university in a single season.

Unfortunately, I have seen many coaches in college athletics succumb to the extreme pressure to win and adopt a "win at all costs" mentality. This approach often came at the expense of the young student-athletes who are verbally and sometimes physically abused. Many have reported being denied everything from water breaks to meal money; some are forced to practice through concussions, serious injuries, and for longer hours than set protocols mandated.

Leaders intrinsically know how critical the S-Motivator of SECURITY is, so much so that the power and ego-obsessed will manipulate others by threatening to dismantle or remove protections. Conversely, the empathic leader uses this knowledge for good, realizing the ability to assure a sense of SECURITY in others is the best way to earn trust, loyalty, obedience, and productivity. For Coach Yourdon, the very thing he feared became his self-sabotaging reality. For all the wins he was able to produce in the game of sport, it was the losses in the game of life that he will sadly be best remembered.

Why SECURITY is So Important

With the majority of the United States working population living within very tight financial limitations and inflation threatening these strained scenarios, stress is real. Post COVID-19, we are seeing record breaking stress and mental illness statistics. Layoffs are also critically high. Social Security and Medicare benefits are constantly in the news as some lawmakers push to get rid of these historically helpful programs. The cost of eggs and gas is high, and toilet paper unpredictably runs low. (Don't ever forget about the toilet paper!) Families are struggling with sick children or elderly parents, and they are all trying to juggle the demands of their jobs. Some are dealing with cancer or other undisclosed illnesses or disability themselves.

Feelings of insecurity are a struggle for the American worker, so they look to leadership for SECURITY. What will you offer? People with a strong SECURITY S-Motivator typically have big responsibilities, or financial or health concerns. Personally, I did not always have a strong SECURITY motivator, but as I got older, nearing retirement age, I became a lot more focused and motivated by my financial picture and the creature comforts of stability. The thought of picking up and moving for a job or anything else at this stage of my life causes me to have a severe allergic reaction! I'm a lot less adventurous now. I am motivated by opportunities that make me feel comfortable, stable, and secure, and I apply greater wisdom to be sure I'm not being sold on something that isn't going to grant me that SECURITY.

While the SECURITY S-Motivator is not limited to older adults, I have discovered there is a higher likelihood that people with this S-Motivator are of an older generation. Many "seasoned" workers my age find themselves taking care of elderly parents, experiencing greater health concerns, or helping their children get on their feet as young adults. They want real help, honest answers, and sincere empathy from you, their fearless leader. Therefore, you must deeply embrace how lacking a sense of SECURITY is one of the greatest sources of workplace conflict for them and others who deem a stable, safe, and secure environment to be most critical to their wellbeing.

Also understand it isn't just the threat of job or financial loss, but also the intangibles of mood, morale, and the feelings of going nowhere, having no future, experiencing no growth, and not winning that stir up conflict and fear. Without SECURITY in place, you will be leading in a culture of negativity with low morale and slow or no progress or productivity.

There are two fundamental reasons why SECURITY is such a strong workplace motivator. The first is based on *psychological need*. The second is how we strange human beings naturally deal with fear and *self-protection*. To be an empathic leader, you must know a little about the science of the brain and how people are naturally inclined to think and act.

- *Psychological Need:* In 1943, psychologist Abraham Maslow introduced the world to his theory of human motivations. Air, food, water, and shelter all appear at the base of Maslow's pyramid of foundational psychological needs. At the next level up the pyramid, you will find things like personal security, job security, health, and resources. It's easy to understand why preservation of these survival and safety needs motivate us to act positively and responsibly. It should also be easy to understand why these needs being threatened, taken, or manipulated by others would cause major stress, conflict, and all-out war!

- *Self-Protection:* Human beings are hard-wired with survival instincts. In our brains, the amygdala is constantly at work ensuring that our fight or flight responses kick in when danger or threats abound. Thus, we are naturally apprehensive, and we fear things (and people) we do not recognize or understand. Since our brains are wired to be in protection mode, you can never underestimate the need for SECURITY as a driving force of what motivates people into action. It is up to you, as the leader, to help guide those naturally fearful or negative actions to become positive ones.

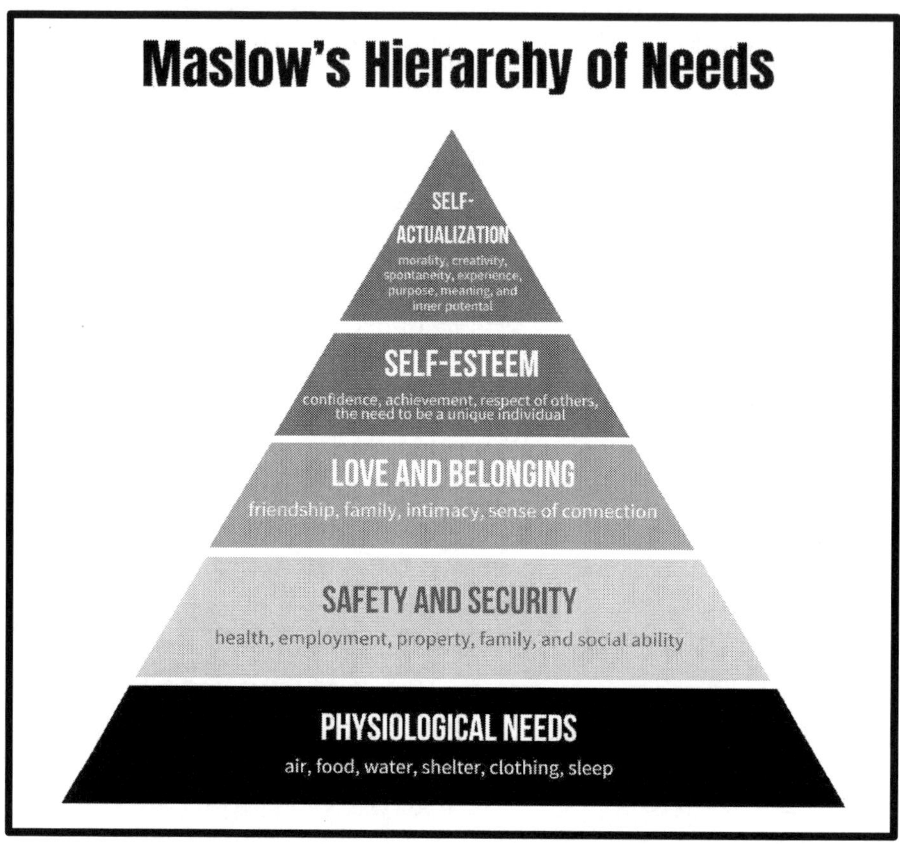

In the workplace, you must address your team's SECURITY needs strategically and proactively. Realize that many people are more apt to think about what they don't have or may lose if they are not influenced or led to think about what they do have or may gain. The smallest uncertainties and doubts can quickly grow into the greatest fears. Thus, when communicating to your team, always remember to include the big picture, future goals, and exciting plans. For example, you may say something like, "We are moving in a very positive direction and I'm trusting a bonus will be in line for us all if we hit our objectives." You may also have to remind them in subtle ways how their needs are being met, such as, "I'm thankful we have a great health benefits package, as my son was able to get the medical care he needed."

To lead effectively, you must provide, not prevent, SECURITY. Ask yourself, "What am I (or what is the leadership team) doing to help people feel physically and emotionally safe in this environment?" You must constantly be aware of your workplace culture, evaluating it with questions like, "Are we requiring too much work? Making too many demands? Offering too little money, time, health benefits, or work-life balance?" Today's workers, more than ever, are hyper-aware of what they need to be secure. Undoubtedly, turnover will be high, and performance will be low when these basic human needs are compromised. Your job, as an empathic leader, is to be a consistently positive, forward thinker, and to be quick to react when you recognize a conflict with SECURITY exists. The following case studies provide examples.

Case Study 3
"Judge Claire Roti"

Complaints of workload stress, fear of termination, and grumblings of wanting to quit all caught Judge Claire Roti by surprise. She considered herself to be a very empathic and fair leader, so she was concerned about what was happening to her workplace culture. In the challenging demands of presiding over legal battles and rewriting laws for fairness and equity, she overlooked the perceptions of fairness, security, and equity that led to low employee morale within her own team and walls of work.

My team surveyed her employees and facilitated open and honest conversations. While Judge Clair's staff held her in high esteem, they had no true idea of who she was as a regular, compassionate human being. People respected Judge Claire out of fear, which stemmed from knowing she expected excellence. But she did not communicate that expectation with empathy. In fact, she lacked a relational connection with her staff, which made them feel insecure. They then inserted their own penal code of what would happen to them if they fell short of expectations.

We helped Judge Claire Roti gain clarity on how having more individual, face-to-face talks with her staff and demonstrating an open-door approach could help quell these insecurities. We helped her see how a simple "Good morning. Tell me how things are going. Share with me some of your challenges or concerns," from the high bench could help eliminate a defensive culture.

The judge took complete accountability and acted swiftly. She began by addressing the staff as a group and inviting them to ask hard questions and express difficult challenges, thoughts, and emotions. She also asked that each member stop by her office for some one-on-one time, and said that she would make a more conscious effort to do the same with them. She stressed that it was important that each of them felt secure with her and with the important roles they played. Within six months, morale in the department changed dramatically for the better, and the next employee engagement survey confirmed the results.

Case Study 4
"Maura Trust" (The Marriott – Starwood Merger)

On April 8, 2016, stockholders of both Marriott International and Starwood Hotels & Resorts Worldwide approved their anticipated merger that closed with the Federal Trade Commission on September 23, 2016. Of course, a merger of this magnitude came with feelings of job uncertainty.

Maura Trust called me to conduct a workshop with one of the regional office divisions. Fear of job layoffs during the restructuring was causing strife, as well as feelings of territorialism, silos, and other change-management scenarios they wanted to avoid.

We set up a team building session that focused on creativity, communication, collaboration, and innovation. We also allotted time for group discussions of existing personal feelings about the changes. Maura proactively allowed workers to voice their concerns. She empathically understood how change tends to heighten people's doubt and anxieties. She also understood the importance of focusing the team on future growth and opportunities, as this is one of the best ways to quell insecurities. An empathic leader understands that what people need when the future feels uncertain is hope and direction of an exciting future, and a chance to imagine and voice how they would like to see things unfold. Maura Trust was the epitome of this type of leader.

While the merger was destined to force changes through restructuring, those changes could have proven disastrous without Maura's empathic leadership. She knew she needed to show compassion for people who indeed may be forced into layoffs, into a different position and responsibilities, or perhaps some who would have to change cities or physical locations. We live in an age of powerful social media, where a company's reputation can be destroyed with one viral post. Failure to proactively demonstrate a prioritization of concern for employees' wellbeing typically leads to unpredictably high conflict costs and chaos.

To empathically lead with SECURITY means you must remember this: *the SECURITY you create for others today is the foundation for everything you wish to build for the future.* To do this, you need to be clear, consistent, and compassionate.

- **Clearly** communicate benefits and expectations of the receipt of those benefits and resources so that everyone understands their roles and rewards. Be transparent with rewards and benefits. It is common to forget all the many things we have to be grateful for or things we have to look forward to. Also be sure to orchestrate a focus on the future when you see people are stuck in negativity or fear.

- **Consistently** monitor distrust and insecurities that may surface within your team. You need a high degree of emotional intelligence so you can critically think of ways to be proactive by considering potential feelings and perceptions for given conflict scenarios. Try not to overthink things, however. Paralysis by analysis is a common problem for leaders trying so hard to get things right. You don't creep over to the extinguisher or analyze the best way to angle it when attempting to put out a fire.

- **Compassionately** keep an open-door policy that allows others to see you as approachable and trustworthy. Instead of making up their own worst-case scenarios, people can simply ask you questions and find confidence in your answers. As hard as it may be at times, remain calm and caring when fear and insecurities surface. And under no circumstances should you ever use threats.

Finally, be self-aware enough to check for your own "stank face," which is my term for when your countenance is wearing fear, frustration, failures, and fouls. People follow your lead in attitude as well as in action. Having a coach, mentor, or great support system is helpful. Also, take steps to stay spiritually and emotionally grounded. Helping others feel secure when you may be struggling with insecure feelings yourself is challenging. That's why you need to take great care of you! Be an example of good physical and mental health. Know when it's time to ask for help.

You, too, deserve compassion and understanding, and to feel secure that everything will work out as it should.

Wrapping Up SECURITY

In the face of adversity, trust building begins with helping people feel safe and secure in who you are and what you (and the organization) will provide. Psychological need and self-protection are natural forces at work in all of us. When people feel threatened, these destructive motivators can become natural disasters for your leadership efforts. You must learn to appeal to and operate from the peace and calm that we all seek and that which we are all capable of performing at our best. You cannot control every complaint, grievance, or discontent, but you can provide an empathic framework for a culture that keeps them to a minimum.

While some people are driven by SECURITY more than others, this motivator is basic, even primitive, in everyone. Fortunately, you can always spot signs when people feel insecure or stressed in their workplaces. Beware of cynicism as well as the quiet quitting. Learn the difference between true agreement and yielding. Be clear, consistent, and compassionate in your leadership, placing faith over fear in times of adversity. Most important, remember that one of the best ways to combat adversity and insecurity is to focus your team forward, projecting how their commitment and contributions today will return the rewards and stability they seek for tomorrow. Show them the ways you can relate to their SECURITY concerns and remind them of the ways they can trust you and their desired provisions to be there for them. (Sidebar: this might include providing toilet paper!)

Be secure in yourself that you are the empathic leader your organization needs to provide the stability and SECURITY that helps teams thrive in tough times. You can. You will.

SECURITY AAA Exercise

Awareness

One of the best ways to develop an understanding of the empathy required to offer SECURITY is to understand the more common reasons people experience workplace stress. The National Institute of Occupational Safety and Health (NIOSH) has identified these following key stressors:[7]

- **The Design of Tasks**. Heavy workload, infrequent rest breaks, long work hours and shiftwork; hectic and routine tasks that have little inherent meaning, do not utilize workers' skills, and provide little sense of control.

- **Management Style.** Lack of participation by workers in decision-making, poor communication in the organization, lack of family-friendly policies.

- **Interpersonal Relationships.** Poor social environment and lack of support or help from coworkers and supervisors. (This is particularly important for remote work scenarios.)

- **Work Roles.** Conflicting or uncertain job expectations, too much responsibility, too many "hats to wear."

- **Career Concerns.** Job insecurity and lack of opportunity for growth, advancement, or promotion; rapid changes for which workers are unprepared.

- **Environmental Conditions.** Unpleasant or dangerous physical conditions such as crowding, noise, air pollution, or ergonomic problems.

Accountability

- Which of the factors cited are relevant to your workplace or current organizational conditions?

- How many of these factors do you experience or have ever experienced?

---

[7] "National Institute for Occupational Safety & Health." Centers for Disease Control and Prevention, www.cdc.gov/niosh/.

- How can those experiences help you feel greater empathy for others?

- What proactive ways can you communicate or take action to help offer a greater sense of SECURITY for your team?

Action

Choose one, two, or all three of these exercises

1) This week, ask your team members what helps them feel secure. Ask them to be specific, painting a clear picture of what peace and stability look and feel like at work. You can even do this as a group icebreaker exercise using pictures from the internet that signify peace or SECURITY. Encourage a discussion of how to create a culture that delivers these things, or how to continue growing feelings of SECURITY at work.

2) Refer to Maslow's Hierarchy of Needs Pyramid. Engage in a discussion around the different levels and how each person's roles and responsibilities in the organization or on the team do or do not relate to the pyramid.

3) Use the Awareness list (or other applicable job stressors) to take a quick survey using a 1-10 rating scale, with 10 being a condition that causes maximum stress. For any element identified as high, say 7 or above, talk about ideas to improve. Ask for specific ways you, as a leader, can help your team feel more secure. Also share what makes you feel secure. Allowing yourself to appear open and vulnerable sets the stage for future candidness and trust.

Your position as an empathic leader is to have a provisional mindset and to be aware of when team insecurities arise. The goal is to first be preventative, but in the case where conflict has already arisen, you must meet insecurities head-on with compassion and optimism before they become problematic for you and the organization. You got this!

CHAPTER 6

SOLUTIONS

My father had a favorite saying that he told me whenever I was complaining or feeling down or frustrated with something. He'd mumble the same sentiment while simultaneously shaking his head watching politics on the nightly news. "Stop celebrating the problem and start celebrating the solution!" He'd add, "If you're not part of the solution then you are part of the problem." This was Dad's way of suggesting that the time we spend moaning, groaning, complaining, and dancing around problems could instead be invested in the ideas, strategies, and actions to solve the problems. My dad was an innovative and accomplished, left-brained, civil engineer who had a passion for problem solving and building anew. He was also extremely generous, kind, and compassionate in his own reserved way.

I imagined Ricky's leaders to be a lot like my dad—critical thinkers who always looked for solutions. In Ricky's case, it would be solutions for training and managing an employee with a cognitive disability. His leaders likely recognized the potential for a multitude of problems or challenges. However, because they led with empathy, they knew the solution was not to deny Ricky a chance based on what he could not do, but to discover opportunities for Ricky to serve based on what he could do. If they had spent too much time "celebrating" potential problems, Ricky may never have had the opportunity to push carts or anything else. That would have been leadership based on fear. Instead, Ricky's leadership was based on faith that for every problem, there was a committed team, strong, wise, and determined enough to find solutions.

The true empathic leader does not exclusively make this deep, comprehensive, empathic, critical thinking investment just with a person with a cognitive disability, but rather with *all people,* because every person's orientation and needs are different. To truly be an empathic leader, you need to understand how each person comes with their own set of physical, emotional, financial, ethical, social, intellectual, or other challenges. Inexperienced or lazy leaders have a bad habit of grouping every person and every problem into a one-size-fits-all solution, only to become frustrated when their employees or team underperform. The more in-tune a leader is with each individual person, the more effective decision-making and problem-solving will be.

I remember my first true professional leadership position. At the young age of twenty-three, still working on my master's degree, I wore the title of Sales and Promotions Manager at a small radio station. I had three salespeople working with me. I say "with me," not "for me," because I never felt like the "boss" let alone their supervisor. They were all my age peers. I thought a "boss" was a disgruntled older person who drank too much coffee and told people what to do. Thrust into a leadership position with basically zero training, I was clueless on the inside but determined to be very in-charge on the outside. I acted like I knew everything, and since I had a background in theatre, I was darn good at it, too! Full transparency, I dreaded every minute of that charade.

At the time, my only true leadership skill was to dive in and lead by example—even if the example was dead wrong! I was wise enough to ask questions, but I'm not sure I always listened to the various answers. If those answers differed from my own, I sometimes perceived it as a threat rather than a benefit to my wisdom and growth to solve problems through diverse ideas. Back then, I had no clue what the power of empathy and perspective-taking could do to help my young team feel more secure, innovative, engaged, and productive. We eventually learned and grew together, and we found solutions to both simple and complex problems.

But the bumps and bruises it took to get there still sting today. Hindsight burns like rubbing alcohol as I compose the very book that could have saved my coworkers and me from so many problems that begat more problems because of my empathic leadership inexperience.

More transparency: as I write this, I am cringing and rolling my eyes. If only you could sense my agonizing sighs of nostalgic embarrassment. Is it too late for me to apologize to my team and my clients now? I'm wondering if I could send them all a copy of this book to make amends. I digress. Fortunately, I know a lot more today than I did then about creating a culture of SOLUTIONS built on empathy and the people who are strongly driven by this S-Motivator. Experience had to be my great teacher.

If SOLUTIONS is your S-Motivator, you likely desire….

- ✓ Working "smart"—practically, logically, consistently, and effectively
- ✓ Leadership that is intelligent, consistent, reliable, organized, and innovative
- ✓ Challenging opportunities to solve complex problems
- ✓ Strategic approaches and innovative discussions
- ✓ Working with/for an organization that is known to be efficient and reputable
- ✓ Being depended on for no-nonsense functional and reliable deliverables
- ✓ Alone time to think, analyze, create, organize, and figure things out
- ✓ Processes and systems that make things better for others

If you are leading people with a strong SOLUTIONS S-Motivator, here is what they seek from you:

- ✓ Respect and understanding of how important it is for them to achieve goals
- ✓ Focused direction that supports their desire to be efficient and get things right
- ✓ Tools and resources to complete tasks and feel accomplished

✓ Patience for their needed time to analyze and process things logically and systematically

✓ Activities that stimulate critical or creative thinking, and autonomy when needed

✓ Constructive criticism and clear communication that helps them solve problems

✓ Opportunity to demonstrate their processes, ideas, organization, or problem solving

✓ Leadership by example of being open, fair-minded, caring, and intelligent

What Happens When You Don't Serve Up SOLUTIONS?

Without the ability to effectively develop and engage people in a culture of SOLUTIONS, you and your organization will not grow to your full potential. You and your team will waste a lot of time celebrating rather than solving problems. This "celebration" comes in the form of a team complaining about what they are not getting, rather than focusing on what they are there to be giving. Not only will morale be poor, but so will your products and services, your customer base, your reputation, your processes, and your future vision, mission, and goals achievement.

People who are strongly motivated by SOLUTIONS find it difficult to work around others who are not, especially if the culture is at a standstill of complaints and grievances. These S-Motivated types thrive on being able to use their innovation and critical thinking skills to be an asset as problem solvers and game changers. They want to get busy addressing real issues, and they are frustrated and deflated when they are in environments that do not support the ability to focus on the problem or task at hand. Because they are logical problem solvers, they are quick to reason when it is illogical to stay. You will then be facing unexpected turnover that includes some of your best thinkers and workers.

You most likely characterize many of the SOLUTIONS-motivated people on your team as highly intelligent, practical, efficient, or conscientious. They have a penchant for seeking knowledge, researching, debating, and philosophizing. When you know how and when to engage them, they will respect and admire you. When you don't, these intelligent and efficient people become your worst critics on anonymous employee feedback surveys. This is particularly true for the more introverted who feel it is valuable to communicate their truth, but do not find it logical or comfortable to do so face-to-face.

People with a strong SOLUTIONS S-Motivator become unmotivated to contribute if you do not regularly include them in what they are most passionate about. You also need to know how much work is enough to keep them engaged without overloading them. When dealing with highly efficient teams or specific, talented team members, many leaders inadvertently default to dumping everything in this team's or person's lap. They are so efficient that the leader can lean on them too much. As a result, burnout is common if you're not mindful of their limitations.

Finally, as a conflict resolution coach, I would be remiss if I didn't stress that when you are not effectively managing a SOLUTIONS-oriented team, you will experience strong personality conflicts. If you don't alleviate these people problems quickly, your team will get lost finding fault with others instead of celebrating solutions that move the business forward. Recent studies show that nearly 50% workplace conflict is due to personality clashes.[8] So, your problem-solving toolkit must include empathic conflict resolution strategies. Employee tensions with each other, and sometimes with your leadership, will be evidenced by cliques and silos, poor communication, and ineffective collaboration. Of course, you can't avoid people problems at work as they are ultimately business problems. However, your inability to lead in these scenarios could prove to be the nightmare that keeps you from achieving your leadership dreams.

---

[8] "Workplace Conflict Statistics 2023: Pollack Peacebuilding." Pollack Peacebuilding Systems, 1 Dec. 2023, pollackpeacebuilding.com/workplace-conflict-statistics/.

Case Study 1
"Seymour Peace"

Seymour Peace owns his own Financial Planning company. They are a tight knit team, and their small, independent company has done well for about a dozen years. But then Seymour's two lead representatives started having personality clashes that made meetings tense and unproductive. Each employee complained about the other to him. Seymour wanted them to grow up, toughen up, and get along. As such, he often avoided getting involved or tried to turn a blind eye or deaf ear to what was going on between them. His avoidance made matters worse, as now the employees weren't just upset with each other, but with him, too, for not leading effectively to help fix their problems.

Seymour failed to adequately plan how to manage conflict until it was hurting his team and his bottom line. The small company's biggest client departed because of the discrepancies that had manifest from these adversarial employees. Meetings were dreadfully uncomfortable, with everyone walking on eggshells as the two exchanged passive aggressive and sometimes blatantly combative jabs.

At first Seymour blamed their immaturity. However, a moment of empathic enlightenment led him to understand that if he, as the leader, was unable to offer a solution, why would he assume they were any more capable of such conflict resolution? Seymour's eventual solution was that everyone needed to be equipped with some conflict resolution strategies. He also decided that he personally needed to learn how to become a better mediator for future personality clashes, to turn destructive conversations into constructive ones.

Leaders must know when they need coaching or help, especially in matters of managing conflict. They need to know that asking for help isn't just okay—it's imperative! Finally, they need to develop confidence as well as courage to face problems rather than fear them. Sometimes the biggest problem leaders will ever experience is believing they don't need help and that problems will eventually go away on their own.

Case Study 2
"Della Gaite"

Della, the Coordinating Manager for a small transportation company, had many responsibilities, including hiring and managing the schedules for other drivers and often serving as a driver herself. Although the driver position was described as "on-call," Della often ran into regular problems with getting her drivers to work on time, if at all. I listened earnestly as one of these drivers, Dan, a very SOLUTIONS-oriented guy, complained about how inefficient and "stupid" Della was. He believed that she caused her own problems by not organizing her schedule in advance to include a systematic rotation of drivers. Worse, she often presented an unprofessional attitude when things fell apart and workers were unavailable.

I listened as Dan rattled off a handful of logistical ways of how Della could solve what he deemed to be very simple problems. "No wonder they can't keep regular drivers!" he exclaimed with conviction. I asked if he had ever shared these ideas with Della. He said he had not and was quite reticent to do so, as he felt Della, as the leader, should be asking her drivers for their input rather than him confronting her. He surmised she did not ask because she already thought she knew what was best. He then showed me three different online Google reviews where Della showed up by name as being unprofessional in her managing role. SOLUTIONS-driven people are natural research types. They are also quick to create their own critical narrative when information is lacking.

I shared with Dan the importance of recognizing that not all leaders know how to ask for help. And since he seemed to have great solutions, I emphasized that he could prove to be an asset if he shared his ideas with Della rather than condemned her privately. If she was open to his suggestions, he would be taking a huge step towards leadership himself. If his doubts about Della proved to be right, I told him he could refer her to me for a quick class in driving SOLUTIONS empathically! (Sidebar: Offering viable solutions to a SOLUTIONS-motivated person is a great way to gain trust and respect.) Dan is still working for Della six months later, and he told me things have improved significantly!

Why SOLUTIONS is So Important

All in favor of following someone who has no clue what they are doing, where they are going, and isn't very knowledgeable, raise your hand. As expected, unanimously all hands are down. Of course, we all want knowledgeable, SOLUTIONS-oriented leaders. One of the main reasons we follow or listen to anyone is because we believe they can help us with our pain points and problems. We rarely think about our need for leadership when things are comfortable. It's only during challenges that suddenly we are ready to seek solutions, listen to ideas, trust advice and guidance, or follow examples.

SOLUTIONS-driven cultures keenly prevent disasters and confidently play the role of clean-up when disasters do happen. Life with no SOLUTIONS means no relief from pain, no cure for complications, and ultimately no progress. Poor leadership is most obvious when the company culture has far more problems than SOLUTIONS. Who or what caused the problem may often be debatable. However, who failed to find the solution to remedy the problem will always find its way back to "who was in charge." The leader bears this burden of blame. In essence, you help yourself as the leader most when you empower problem solving in others.

Please don't misinterpret this burden of blame. You may think being SOLUTIONS-driven means you need to be autonomous and do everything yourself. However, part of being knowledgeable is accepting you do not have all the answers all the time. Surrounding yourself with SOLUTIONS-oriented people, developing a SOLUTIONS-oriented culture, and delegating accordingly is important because it is what's expected from the leader. But it takes a great deal of empathy to do it well.

Maintaining a true culture of SOLUTIONS is essential because it epitomizes the significance of diversity and inclusion. The very people who challenge you with differing opinions, play the role of devil's advocate, and push back to make you uncomfortable force you to dig deeper to find truth. They are the game changers who consistently help you win when it comes to progress and innovation. As the empathic leader, you must remember this when you are being pushed, and when you are constructively challenging others or giving feedback.

Recognizing people's problem-solving strengths is a keen skillset in achieving the culture of SOLUTIONS that drives businesses forward. Some people will be great at solving people-related problems, such as Human Resources professionals, nurses, and counselors. Some are better at processes and tasks, like engineers, accountants, and IT personnel. Others have the gift of being great at both. Your role as the empathic leader is to care enough to identify, develop, and engage these strengths to empower the critical, innovative, and creative capacities of all. Your team or organization will thrive because of it.

Case Study 3
"CARL ONMEY"

To date, I have never met anyone who is as intuitive and relentless at problem solving as Carl Onmey. He appeared reserved and "cucumber cool" to the casual observer, until a problem came along or something needed to be fixed or finished. Then he became a fast-acting, high-strung, Energizer Bunny! He could be anywhere, even casually hanging out, and sense when a problem was about to happen. Out the corner of his eye he would see a protruding electrical cord in a restaurant or some other potential danger, and he would stop all conversation, jump up and tell the manager, or take care of the problem himself if no one acted fast enough. Carl was already processing a solution in his mind by the time most people were just figuring out something had gone wrong.

A military veteran, Carl found satisfying work for one of our United States government defense agencies. His director took special notice of Carl's unique and uncanny gifts and promoted him to a position created just for him—a logistics analyst position where he was called on regularly to use his problem-solving gifts and ingenuity. I listened with respect and admiration as Carl beamed with pride at what the promotion meant to him, how fond he was of his job, and how impressed he was with his leadership and highly intelligent and cohesive team. I asked what he liked most. He said, "They let me do my thing." In a nutshell, Carl knew his gifts and he knew he did not need micro-managing, but freedom to solve problems, think of new ways to make things better for others, and to be proactive, promotional, persistent, and proficient.

The interesting thing about the empathy required to relate and lead someone with a SOLUTIONS S-Motivator is many of them have already worked out their own needs and motivation. When they recognize that you know and respect their skills and knowledge, and you empower them to get the job done, they see you as the smart leader, too. This leaves you time to dedicate to those who may require more development and attention, or to empower other SOLUTIONS-oriented team members to grow through mentoring and leading others.

Case Study 4
"Noah Moore"

Since its inception, Google has fascinated me. I can only imagine what it would take to be an empathic leader employing SOLUTIONS in an organization relentless for its search for better answers; a place where being a know-it-all is not a criticism to be avoided, but an expectation to be admired! Somewhere in the organization is an exemplary leader. I'll call him **Noah Moore** (because I can't help being clever), whose leadership job is to manage and motivate countless SOLUTIONS-driven teammates. Noah knows that it's not what one individual knows, but the consistent involvement of individuals and teams that clearly defines SOLUTIONS for their culture and for their customers.

Empathically embracing and managing diverse perceptions and people's need for answers has been at the core of Google's global success. Additionally, having a clear mission fueled by people motivated by the rewards of problem-solving and achievement is what helped this company become what I believe to be a prime example of empathic leadership with great attention to SOLUTIONS. I googled what makes a leader great at Google. (Kind of ironic, right?) This is what I found:

- Is a good coach.
- Empowers team and does not micromanage.
- Creates an inclusive team environment, showing concern for success and well-being.
- Is productive and results oriented.
- Is a good communicator—listens and shares information.
- Supports career development and discusses performance.
- Has a clear vision/strategy for the team.
- Has key technical skills to help advise the team.
- Collaborates across the org/dept.
- Is a strong decision maker.

This is the making of a SOLUTIONS-focused leader at a highly SOLUTIONS-focused company. Noah Moore certainly has to be intelligent to be a great leader at Google. But he coaches, empowers, communicates, supports, advises, collaborates, and makes decisions not for himself, but for *others*. Every leader does. That is why empathy is not an option. It is in and of itself the solution.

To empathically lead with SOLUTIONS means you must constantly develop critical thinking and creative problem-solving skills. This may sound like a shameless self-plug, and perhaps it is, but finding a coach is a great way to stay on top of your problem-solving game. According to an article in *Forbes*, the coaching industry is expected to grow at a compound annual rate of 7.6% by 2026.[9] The popularity of coaching continues to grow in part because its efficacy does as well. Coaching provides a viable resource for leaders who want to sound things out and grow in their self-awareness. Coaching particularly helps entrepreneurs and small business leaders who are looking for solutions to new and emerging challenges.

As a leader, you will undoubtedly have many days where solving problems feels like the only thing you do. Problems are inevitable. That's why you must embrace problems as "challenges to be conquered," and not allow the challenges to conquer you. The inability to persevere to find solutions or "play through fouls" creates even greater problems. Effectively leading to stimulate a culture of SOLUTIONS means you must embrace the SOLUTIONS mindset first before you can effectively develop the skillset. You must have courage to face adversity or difficulties before you develop the confidence to overcome them. Then you must develop that same mindset and skillset in others. Problem-solving does not have to equate to stress or pressure. Remember that pressure builds in closed spaces, not open ones, so stay open to diverse ideas and people in order to create a team environment of problem solvers.

---

[9] Laker, Benjamin. "Every Leader Can Benefit from Coaching. Here's Why." Forbes Magazine, 4 Oct. 2022, www.forbes.com/sites/benjamin-laker/2022/10/04/every-leader-can-benefit-from-coaching-heres-why/.

Finally, remember to adapt the "No Stank Face" approach when it comes to problems. You can be realistic about the difficulty of the challenge without coming across as defeated. Stay positive in your team's ability to find solutions. Knowing that problems cause conflict often drives many of us to be problem-solvers. But this knowledge also drives many people to be problem avoiders. The fact is that problems cause confusion, frustration, and sometimes anger and hurt. Our countenance wears this even when our words do not. So, keep in mind, sometimes the simplest answer is to remain optimistic that things will work out if you remain determined to celebrate the SOLUTIONS and not the problems.

Wrapping Up SOLUTIONS

Your team wants to know you are intelligent and capable, as those are attractive leadership qualities. However, one of the biggest mistakes for new leaders (and a big reason why imposter syndrome can become so daunting) is believing that you must be smart enough to solve every problem by yourself. In reality, you have SOLUTIONS-oriented people on your team who are driven to be innovative, fact finding, analytical, and process and problem focused. They need to know you trust them, you include them, and you allow them to take the lead in some capacity to find SOLUTIONS.

If you are a do-it-yourself leader, your inability to delegate invalidates your staff members, and they won't be motivated to work as effectively as they are capable. Additionally, they may go into judgment mode and become critical of your leadership for not doing things as smartly, efficiently, or as effectively as they believe it should be done. Therefore, learn to delegate and play to your team's strengths. To do this, you must truly know your leadership team and your staff overall. What kind of problems are they best at solving? Who are your most critical thinkers? Who is great with people? Who struggles with conflict resolution? You will solve problems more effectively and efficiently with this empathic knowledge, and it will certainly help prevent any imposter syndrome you may experience.

Finally, always be leery of personality clashes in the workplace. It's human nature for people to disagree at times. But that is a good thing.

Diverse perspectives give us the greatest opportunities for growth. Your resilience and example will empower others to stay positive in the face of problems and to be committed to finding SOLUTIONS. Additionally, because of your empathy you will care enough to understand what drives people to be their best, even through the worst of problems and challenges. You will coach them to find the SOLUTIONS for the win, and you will stay at the top of your game by surrounding yourself with SOLUTIONS-driven people, including a coach or mentor of your own. I know a bona fide "SOLUTIONS Celebrater" when you're ready!

SOLUTIONS AAA Exercises

Awareness

Are you a strong problem solver? How do you know? What approach(es) do you regularly use or prefer? These are important questions to ask yourself to understand your capacity to solve problems. Consider this quick self-evaluation tool to get a clearer picture.

How do you rank yourself in these six areas: (1 – Low; 5 – High):

1) Drive/Ambition – the desire to solve problems to accomplish goals
2) Persistence/Perseverance – the ability to push through challenges and setbacks
3) Intelligence – critical thinking, creativity, as well as wisdom and common sense
4) Empathy – caring and concern for others' feelings and perspectives
5) Optimism – faith or belief in positive outcomes
6) Strategy – skills to analyze situations and then develop and implement a plan

Accountability

Once you self-evaluate, consider asking others on your team how they see you as a problem solver. In what ways? Strengths? Areas of Improvement? Discuss with a coach or mentor a plan to develop in the areas you need to target. You can be more specific with your goals by focusing on process-oriented problem solving vs. people-oriented problem solving. Identify others on the team who are stronger where you are weaker (or vice-versa) and strategize ways to help each other be accountable for growth.

Action

This week, or in your next planning meeting, discuss diverse ways for solving problems. Implement the following team-building session to focus on how to grow in the area of SOLUTIONS.

1. Ask your team or staff to evaluate themselves in the six Awareness areas.
2. Discuss collective team strengths and areas of improvement.
3. Using the problem-solving formula provided, or another agreed upon method, target how you will improve your own problem-solving area(s) of improvement.

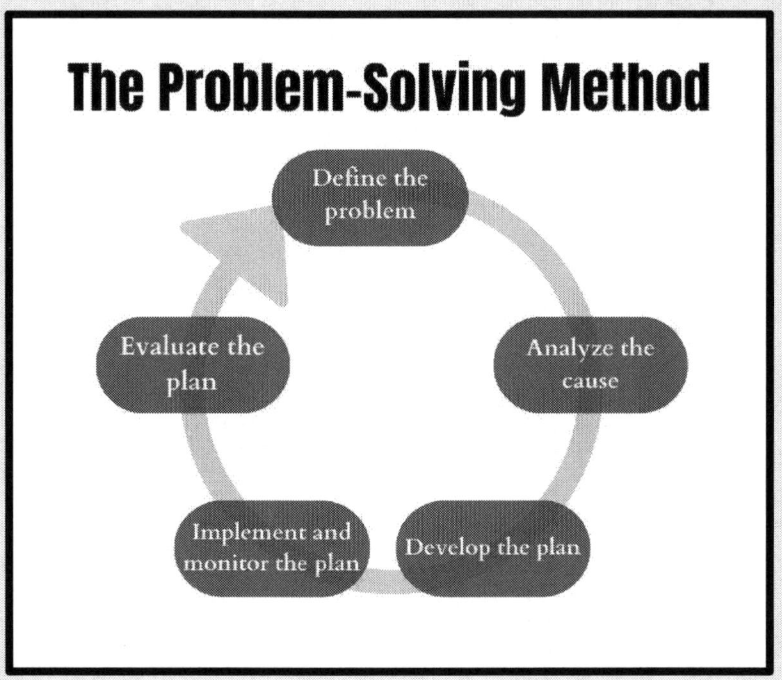

Define the Problem: What is the problem? How significant or severe?

Analyze the Cause: How and why did this problem occur?

Develop the Plan: Consider alternative solutions and challenges to these ideas. Determine what needs to be done, who needs to be involved, when it should be started/finished (timeline), how it will be executed, and what metrics will be used.

Implement and Monitor the Plan: Take action by doing what you plan to do with regular accountability checks to see if plans are being followed as stated.

Evaluate the Plan: Did the plan work? How do you know? (Metrics) What happens next?

CHAPTER 7

STRUCTURE

> *"When structure is solid, freedom and growth become fluid."*
> *—Vera Jones*

Imagine what could have happened if Ricky worked in an environment without STRUCTURE. I won't pretend to know much about Ricky's background or his disability. The one thing I do know is that Ricky was one heck of a cart pusher! I chuckle every time I hear his loud "I GOT IT!" echo in my head. Just thinking about his excitement and enthusiasm warms my spirit. Ricky knew how to push the carts safely in the parking lot. He knew where to stack the empty carts and whom he should assist next. He knew a lot of things we might otherwise take for granted. Such is the case when considering STRUCTURE in an organization or culture. Leaders require a great deal of empathic consideration and forethought to cultivate a reliable system of doing things the best way, for the right reasons, and consistently well.

How many times have you started a new job and felt completely lost, perhaps even overwhelmed, because you lacked knowledge about the people, the plans, the process, and the overall culture? Systems and processes don't always come easy at first. But eventually, from written rules, policies, and procedures to physical training and hands-on experiences, you came to understand these things in your workplace. This is the essence of STRUCTURE. The clearer and more consistent your STRUCTURE is, the more successful the working culture becomes.

Ricky knew exactly how to do a lot of things because he had a leader or leadership team who provided specific guidance and specialized training. They empathically considered all the things Ricky needed to learn and understand about that grocery store, such as their mission to serve their customers, as well as the rules, roles, and responsibilities required to do that well. If Ricky had not received proper training and supervision, can you imagine where some of those carts would have ended up? Or the vehicles that may have been dented or scratched? Add to that the subsequent problems, complaints, or lawsuits that would have resulted and you can clearly see why the leadership team needed to take the time to empathically understand Ricky's orientation, needs, and motivation and uniquely develop him into their established culture. Such STRUCTURE takes a great deal of organized thought and detail to establish.

I admit that when I participated in my own engagement poll, I ranked STRUCTURE as my least motivational. That doesn't mean I deem it unimportant. Trust me, my lack of proper planning and detailed thinking has gotten me into a lot of trouble over the years. I deeply and personally know its significance. To this day, I surround myself with people who have a strong STRUCTURE S-Motivator because I know it is not my driving motivator or strength, but it is critical for success. Interestingly, while I may not be the most detailed-oriented person you'll meet, I do not perform well nor do I enjoy working in environments without plans, processes, rewards, checks and balances, goals, and a vision and mission in place. I have the greatest respect and admiration for people whose analytical brains keenly orchestrate STRUCTURE in the workplace.

I gave my dad a shout out in the SOLUTIONS chapter, so let me show equal love and share a quote from my very structured mom. When I was a child, after about the tenth time in a week she fussed at me to clean my room, she would remind me I should have ***"a place for everything, and everything in its place."*** Even today, when life gets crazy and the laundry backs up in a pile in my closet corner or spends a few extra days relaxing in the dryer, I can hear my lovable mother's adage ringing in my ears. Mom was the most organized "neat freak" I ever knew. She was the best part of the worst part of my unstructured lifestyle. Like many children, I never understood how smart my mother was until all her "I told you so's" resonated in my adult life. Mom deeply lived and breathed STRUCTURE. Because of her, I crave it even though it is not my most evident strength.

Not only was my mother a STRUCTURE motivated person, but my co-consultant of 15 years, who doubles as my best friend, is as well. The same is true for my executive assistant of the past four years. They'd probably be the first to tell you my right-brained style of unbridled "winging it" makes them nuts! They challenge me to grow in the ways I need it most. Their strengths are my weaknesses, and vice versa. So, when it comes to understanding STRUCTURE, its importance in company culture, what STRUCTURE-driven people desire to be at their best, and what happens when they are not led by those who provide a culture of organized, systematic, forward-thinking processes and guidance, you can trust that I have learned these things via the school of hard knocks! Allow me to open the door and soften those knocks for you.

If STRUCTURE is your S-Motivator you likely desire....

- ✓ Common-sense procedures and guidance for how to work in a system
- ✓ Clarity of vision, mission, goals, plans, and direction
- ✓ Consistent organization and instructions to accomplish objectives
- ✓ A culture with systems of accountability and clearly defined roles
- ✓ Leadership that is clear, steady, fair, and follows up
- ✓ Reliability, reasonability, responsibility, and rationality in relationships
- ✓ An organized system in place for resources and rewards
- ✓ Effective governance of rules and regulations and proper discipline

If you are leading people with a strong STRUCTURE S-Motivator, this is what they seek from you...

- ✓ To be clear, consistent, and organized, and allow them to be as well
- ✓ To be sensitive to how crazy it makes them to operate in clutter, chaos, and hurry

- ✓ Clear documentation, presentations, and resources (spreadsheets, videos, handbooks)
- ✓ Clarity in your direction and instruction with minimal change
- ✓ Discussions with time to ask questions for clarity when there is change
- ✓ Opportunities to lead in their own organized method or from behind the scenes
- ✓ Concise and conceptual meetings and assignments that don't waste time
- ✓ Fair rules and procedures with clear consequences that are consistently adhered to

What Happens When You Don't Serve Up STRUCTURE?

In my experiences and research over the past fifteen years, leaders and their teams struggle due to two main reasons: lack empathy and lack of clarity. I have found lack of empathy to be the greatest people problem, while lack of clarity is the greatest process problem. Lack of empathy for people who crave clarity is the double whammy! In fact, lacking both empathy and clarity psychologically damages STRUCTURE-motivated people the most. When leaders fail to understand how consequential their lack of clear and consistent organization, direction, systems, and processes are to the people who are so tremendously STRUCTURE-inclined, the bulk of all productivity can come to a screeching halt.

Think of it this way. You wish to build a house, but your instructions to the builder are vague, such as "Just make it big and fancy." On top of that you add pressure by telling the builder to hurry up because you want to it done quickly and you don't have time to discuss the details. When the builder arrives frustrated and flustered at your next meeting, you ask, "Why did you build it this way?" If you understand STRUCTURE-oriented people even a little bit, you can envision the fire and steam escaping from the builder's eyes and ears! You can also see why that house will never get built. The details are lacking, resulting in frustration, poor productivity, and ultimate failure. This is true whether building a house or leading a culture of workers. Without proper STRUCTURE, things don't get done.

While most of us would never lead with such absurdity as in the house building example, we sometimes fail to comprehend how STRUCTURE-motivated people process things. To them, the picture I created of the home-building scenario feels real and resembles (in their mind) their workplace. Your empathic perspective-taking or predisposition to think on this level will consistently prevent their frustrations. In the builder example, you would know you missed the STRUCTURE boat when you get flooded with more questions about size, shapes, colors, materials, architectural blueprints, codes, regulations, and permits than you could possibly absorb. The STRUCTURE-driven are quick to ask questions most people do not think about. Their critical thinking skills rival that of genius, even if to some extent it feels annoying.

People motivated by STRUCTURE view almost all instruction as our builder does, especially if it is a new project or task. They are those engineers, architects, and administrative gurus of the gang who ask a lot of questions and perceive you to be the most foolish leader on the planet if you offer vague answers or instruction. Loose direction is not welcome in their house. If you lack empathy, you may dismiss these people with thoughts like, "They ask too many questions." Or you may feel like you must explain everything in minute detail. With empathy, you will come to understand this S-Motivation is an absolute need for these workers to experience a functional level of comfort, fueling their desire to get a task right. When you don't fuel their need for knowledge, you cannot properly drive your organization in the right direction.

While more right-brained artist types may appreciate the freedom to imagine and create from scratch and may accept your vagueness with complete license for innovation and ingenuity, people who crave STRUCTURE will immediately dismiss you as incompetent. Their frustration shows up primarily as a barrage of questions. If those questions aren't answered with adequate, clear instruction, you can expect silent unproductivity next, as many internalize rather than vocalize their frustrations. Ultimately, these STRUCTURE-oriented people are likely to exit any environment they deem chaotic or unorganized. Period. They have low tolerance for an environment or a leader that does not respect their need for structure, including a workplace with low accountability for creating, implementing, or consistently following rules and policies.

STRUCTURE S-Motivated people cannot deal with an unorganized boss or an environment that makes them feel they are operating in chaos. Additionally, they take great offense when a leader criticizes how they completed a task, especially if that leader did not take the time to offer clear direction as to how they wanted something done in the first place. STRUCTURE-oriented people prefer clear direction the first time, or at the very least, the empathy and patience to have a discussion to gain that sense of clarity. These are your workers who, like the SOLUTION-driven, want to solve problems, but they need to solve them in a common sense, systematic, process-controlled, procedures written, policies followed, step-by-step, detailed spreadsheet kind of way. Am I clear? Perhaps these case studies will help you remember to be.

Case Study 1
"Will Waite"

Will Waite's resume was impeccable. With a strong military background working for a high-ranking leader, he came into his new position highly recommended. However, a few months into the new job, Will was often late on assignments, forgetful, and seemed to always have too much on his plate. Through one-on-one coaching, I discovered Will was a perfectionist suffering from a clinical level of procrastination. I was curious how this could be given his admirable work history.

I learned that Will was offered a lot of freedom in his new career endeavor. His workplace was laid back, and his boss was easy-going and used to managing a team of efficient self-starters. The workload was time sensitive, but not overly demanding. Due to his perfectionist tendencies, Will likely had a proclivity to procrastinate that was not able to surface under the more military style of leadership he was accustomed to, where everything had a deadline and most tasks had to be completed quickly and consistently. It was detailed and routine work. This new, more laid-back environment gave Will too much time and freedom, something to which he was not accustomed. He never experienced the liberty to create his own structure and he struggled to adapt. He habitually functioned best being told what to do, when to do it, and how to do it, pronto!

While Will Waite's case was one of the more extreme cases I had ever witnessed in terms of individual unproductivity, it helped me learn something important. The freedom and autonomy that are considered luxuries for some could prove disastrous for others. Even though many people proclaim they do not like being micro-managed, an empathic leader must be mindful that this preference is not universal. Some people absolutely need and desire extra detailed meetings, coaching, specific instruction, and follow-up. They may often internalize their frustration when they don't receive it, and the only way you know anything is wrong is when the unproductivity surfaces. By employing empathy to look deeper, you can provide greater STRUCTURE in the form of training, mentoring, regimented timelines, or follow up for them to achieve their best work.

Case Study 2
"Kay Yahtick"

Kay Yatick was an affiliative and democratic style leader. On the surface, she was one of the last you'd assume to lack empathy in any area. She was open-minded and inclusive, often asking questions about what others on the team thought about various strategies and challenges. She always encouraged new concepts and tactics. Because of this, her laissez-faire attitude and style set the stage for long meetings that left a few workers feeling frustrated. Often, Kay did not include an agenda, and if she did it was a loose one, subject to emotional tangents and detours.

Some of the feedback I received in employee interviews pointed to comments like, "Just tell me what you want me to do." Another wrote, "It feels like we meet just to meet. By the time I get to ask my questions, it's time for the meeting to end." In frustration another proclaimed, "I always leave feeling clueless, like every meeting is a complete waste of time." Despite her best intentions and overall empathic leadership style, Kay overlooked how important STRUCTURE was to her team. Her staff thrived on details and data and preferred her to directly address them with her own guidance and points of emphasis, including timelines, clearly defined roles, and time to ask more analytical or detailed questions.

I collaborated with Kay on implementing a consistent meeting structure that included specific and expected time for questions. It also included specific timeline objectives for completion and follow-up. Kay delegated the role of creating the weekly meeting agenda to the most detailed STRUCTURE S-Motivated member on the team, who unbeknown to Kay was also her biggest critic. Meeting time became more efficient, and productivity increased. Kay became a better leader realizing that a little bit of STRUCTURE could indeed go a long way.

Why Structure is So Important

We live in a world of organization, rules, and governance. Even if it is organized chaos, there is still some semblance of structure. And like the water in the well, we miss it when it's completely gone. Most of us work in environments with many of our needed structures in place. Therefore, we often take them for granted. People strongly aligned with a STRUCTURE motivation, however, think of the little details and finer points many people miss. They are the forward thinkers who consider rules, regulations, and governance to live by. They are the stabilizers who maintain necessary documentation, files, data, and systems. They are the critical thinkers who look back, analyze, and conceptualize where things have gone wrong so mistakes don't get repeated. We simply cannot build anything lasting without adequate STRUCTURE.

As an entrepreneur, I learned long ago that the hardest part of any project is getting started. Credit STRUCTURE for that. Figuring out all the details needed to bring an idea to life is difficult, let alone continuously enforcing and tweaking even more details along the way when necessary. For example:

- What are the values, vision, and mission?
- What are the goals?
- What systems or processes do we need to get there?
- Who needs to be involved?
- What will they do?
- How will they do it?
- What do they need?
- What is Plan B when things don't go well?
- How do we determine fairness?
- How will discipline or correction take place?

So many questions need so many answers! Failure to nail down STRUCTURE often proves to be the demise and destruction of many business endeavors. *"Prior proper planning prevents poor performance. Period."*

Trust me, it's easier to say this phrase ten times fast than it is to actually *do* it one time slow.

Even in an age where young workers are screaming, "I want freedom and autonomy," they still need stability, processes, and logistics in place to help them achieve. Never get tricked into believing that allowing people to consistently "wing it" is the best policy. If this was the case, why would any of us need leadership? There is security and consistency that comes from order, processes, training, and overall structure in an organization, just as it is in civilization. We need empathic leaders to recognize and understand the people who are most passionate about getting it right, one detail at a time. As my mom said, things work best when there is a place for everything, and everything is in its place. We all have a place within us that requires the stability STRUCTURE provides.

Case Study 3
"Ben Lyon"

When conducting a workshop with Human Resources personnel, I learned timecard negligence or dishonesty is a common and serious offense in virtually any organization, and many have strict rules and consequences concerning this issue. Still, human beings like to push the envelope on rules, especially if they think they can get away with it. Leaders tend to know this about human behavior and usually can identify the rare bad actors who are more likely to buck the system.

Ben Lyon, however, was the employee one would least suspect. He was found guilty of manipulating his timecard, and his supervisor was painfully surprised by his actions. Ben was an exceptional employee and not known to be dishonest. He knew he was playing with fire and was thankful that his supervisor took an empathic approach to his discipline by at least asking him why he lied. His need for more money for his family was at the root of his deceit (perhaps understandable, but nonetheless unacceptable). Fortunately, the company had clear STRUCTURE in place. While Ben's supervisor had empathy for his financial struggles, he had a responsibility to stay true to the agency's rules and regulations. He also had to stay true to his own values and moral responsibility. Ben accepted his punishment and was deeply apologetic for his actions.

Ben's respect for his supervisor grew because of his commitment to integrity even when Ben failed to live up to his own. What could have been a deviation from proper discipline because his supervisor felt sorry for him proved to be a clearly defined expectation and application of fairness and justice. Empathy in leadership does not equate to an excuse for misdeeds. Policies and rules are put in place for a reason, and in many ways rescue the leader from the stress of having to play the role of judge, jury, and disciplinarian. Rules and consequences that are clear, written, and consistently enforced are the STRUCTURE that alleviates chaos and confusion for all. Chaos- and confusion-free environments are ones we all desire to work and live in.

Case Study 4
"Starbucks, Strong Coffee, and Structure"

On April 12, 2018, Donte Robinson and Rashon Nelson went to a Starbucks Coffee Company store in Philadelphia, PA to meet a business associate. Soon after their arrival, they were escorted out in handcuffs by local police. Their alleged crime was that they had not made a purchase and declined to leave. The video of the incident went viral on social media and suggested the crime was not Robinson's and Nelson's, but rather Starbucks for racism and discrimination. Instant national headlines led to swift public outcry, including protests at various Starbucks locations.

Shocked upon hearing the news, Starbucks' CEO Kevin Johnson was unprepared for the criticism, conversation, and questions that followed. But one thing was clear. He knew his company's value statement was as strong as the coffee they brewed: *Creating a culture of warmth and belonging, where everyone is welcome.* This racially biased incident was threatening the STRUCTURE the company was built upon. Clarity of their mission—*to inspire and nurture the human spirit, one cup, and one neighborhood at a time*—was the foundation of positive change. Having such a simple, clearly defined, written, and advertised mission statement provided unequivocal direction for Starbuck's leadership to take immediate accountability and action.

Johnson flew to Philadelphia and arranged to meet Mr. Robinson and Mr. Nelson in person. "We could not ignore the painful truth: racial bias was at the heart of the incident, and it was reprehensible," he lamented. Johnson likely never imagined he would be dealing with such a challenge. Fortunately, somewhere in the halls of the Starbuck's organization were people with a strong STRUCTURE S-Motivator who had the foresight to know that clearly defined values and a mission statement would provide critical guidance to help leaders identify when there was a crack in the foundation of what Starbucks had intended to build. As a result, Starbucks' leadership was able to take immediate action to repair that which had been broken.

Within 18 months, Starbucks had quickly turned its image around by involving its employees in various diversity, equity, and inclusion trainings and taking a greater public stance on such sensitivities. By doing so, they strengthened their STRUCTURE and commitment to their employees and customers. A scandal that could have become the demise of a less structured company became a resounding, rebounding win for Starbucks.

To empathically lead with STRUCTURE means you must understand and empower fundamental frameworks in both people and processes. The first part of becoming a STRUCTURE-focused leader is learning to think like a builder who has fully embraced the fundamentals of developing people. You cannot achieve this without a proper blueprint that includes defining the vision, mission, plans, values, resources or materials, and goals necessary to take action. What are you doing? Why are you doing it? Who are you doing it with and for? Where are you doing it? How will you do it? What obstacles will you possibly encounter and how will you overcome them? Lots of questions require lots of clear, detailed answers. So be curious and inquisitive. Stimulate critical thinking and intelligence in yourself so you can adequately do so in others.

The second part of becoming a STRUCTURE-focused leader is realizing there are people who think this way all the time, even if you do not, and they function at their best when you empathically appreciate and encourage their analytical and organizational strengths. They are thinkers, builders, strategists, puzzle wizards, policy perfectionists, and administrative champions. Their passion is in the process, and their detailed, "getting things right" approach is the prize for you and everyone else in the organization. They will think through what's needed and accurate for a mission statement. They will assure the employee handbook has considered rule validity as well as how to handle the violations. They will provide the needed analysis for why things fell apart and offer valuable insight as to how to rebuild. There are infinite puzzles to be solved, numbers to be crunched, angles and alternatives to be considered, and they need a sense of structure to figure it all out.

They also need your patience, your time for follow up, and your due diligence to not waste their time with a lack of organization or prior proper planning. Everyone has and can relate to a need for STRUCTURE to some degree, but not all leaders can truly motivate those who inherently breathe and achieve best with it. You need considerable empathy, clarity, and consistency in how you relate and communicate to be an effective leader with this S-Motivated group. Listen actively. Instruct specifically and descriptively. Allow time for questions. Write down goals and policies. Present agendas and plans. Be a good time manager and help others by offering timelines and realistic goals to achieve. Carefully plan for things to operate best, and discuss the valuable lessons learned when they don't. Everyone you lead needs these building blocks from you, and you will grow and develop more than you realize every time you rise to the challenge.

Wrapping Up STRUCTURE

When STRUCTURE is solid, freedom and growth become fluid. People who are motivated or passionate about STRUCTURE typically don't get frustrated by problems. They get frustrated when leadership and teams do not have a logical or systematic plan or process in place to address the problems. STRUCTURE and SECURITY are closely related because operating in an environment with minimal chaos or confusion creates a feeling of safety, low stress, and best operating conditions for success. STRUCTURE and SOLUTIONS are closely related because the many questions that need to be asked require not just any answer, but the right solution to specific problems. So don't be quick to dismiss the inquiries that may come. They are inevitable and necessary.

Whether you are running a large corporation or are an entrepreneur running a small business, you will quickly learn the importance of my mother's adage, "everything in its place, and a place for everything." Our brains as well as our working lives operate best when thoughts and actions are organized and free of clutter and confusion. The value of having well-designed, written plans to serve as a blueprint for whatever you wish to build is immense. They provide protection and provisions and help dreams become reality. The same can be said for those who are so passionately driven by the concept and enforcement of STRUCTURE. They are the architects, builders, and administrators of dreams, and without the capacity to lead them effectively, nothing will work out quite as well as it should. Lead them empathically, and the sky truly is the limit.

STRUCTURE AAA Exercises

Awareness

Based on what you've learned about people with a strong STRUCTURE S-Motivator, can you identify them in your workplace? Social circles? How would you describe them? Do you know what excites them? Have you ever seen them frustrated?

Accountability

Notice I asked a lot of questions here. When you receive a lot of questions from a particular person about how things should work or how things need to be done, this is a clue that you are dealing with a STRUCTURE-motivated person. It may also be a clue that you aren't providing people with enough details or clarity in your communication with them. So, this is a quick self-awareness metric as well as an exercise in empathy.

Speaking of asking, once you identify a STRUCTURE-driven person, be sure to ask them what their preferred method of communication is and whether they find your direction clear. Ask them what you can do to improve. Ask when you can follow up to measure your leadership growth with them. This is a humble and empathic way of connecting with anyone, but particularly people who thrive on details and consistency.

Action

1) Before your next meeting, ask each team member to produce an agenda template for the best way to structure meetings. If time permits, you can also do this as an icebreaker or exercise during your next meeting. Ask about the logic behind why people constructed the agenda the way they did. Generate a discussion and real solutions for improving the way you meet with this exercise. It will not only be fun for your STRUCTURE-oriented folks, but it will also likely improve the way you meet overall moving forward.

2) Ask each person if they know the company's mission. Stimulate conversation about how it is currently being demonstrated in your

department or on your team. Write down the steps involved to improve one aspect of the mission. Commit to a timeline to implement this change. Who will monitor the progress? Will there be a reward? Be specific and help others develop ways to operate with greater STRUCTURE.

CHAPTER 8

SINCERITY

Imagine the look in the grocery store leader's eyes when they told Ricky's parents, "Don't worry. We will take good care of him." Feel the SINCERITY needed to convince a parent to let go and trust that their cognitively disabled child was working for good, kind, and honest people who genuinely cared. Chances are they displayed that same integrity and SINCERITY with all their employees, in the way they stocked their produce and lined their shelves, and in the way they determined pricing and policies. The company's SINCERITY was even evident in the smiling young woman at the checkout register. In fact, I imagine most customers felt a genuine warmth while shopping in this grocery store. I know I did. Ricky screaming "I GOT IT!" while pushing my cart simply sealed the deal. It was like warmth infused with a little electric shock!

This grocery store was small, but it was authentic, welcoming, and honest. I felt their SINCERITY the moment I walked in. I could have gone to the much bigger grocery store four miles away. I usually shopped there as it was closest to my house. Yet, after my first experience at Ricky's store, I had no problem driving the extra ten minutes just so I could experience a dose of this store's SINCERITY. Some prices may have been a little higher, and they stocked fewer item varieties, but even that was not enough to deter me from returning to this little grocery store. In the midst of my grief, at a time when I needed simplicity and peace the most, I found an inviting integrity that kept me coming back.

That's the magic of SINCERITY. It keeps you coming back. You cannot undervalue the power of connection built on honesty, trust, genuineness, and care, whether it's a business or personal relationship. I particularly value honesty, as my parents deeply ingrained it into my value system. My mom and dad were strict on the "you better not cheat, steal, lie—or else" style of parenting. That "or else" part had the power to get me in line just on pure imagination of what might happen should I fall short of the virtues they had set for me. It's been a while since I had a sidebar, so please humor my digression for just a moment…

I was seven years old when my mother and I went to the grocery store one fateful day. I was reluctant to go because Mom liked to shop slowly and I was extra hungry. When we were in the produce aisle, Mom was focused on inspecting, plucking, and shaking cantaloupes to determine which one seemed the freshest. I sighed as my hunger pangs began to bully and taunt me. Suddenly, I eyeballed three grapes lying loose from their little branch in the produce bin. With lightning speed, I grabbed them like jacks in my little hands and popped them into my big mouth. "Yummy!" I thought. But then my heart raced as my stomach churned, and I felt a burst of emotion I had never identified before. It was hot, accusatory, and relentless. For the first time I experienced real guilt and shame.

I stole three grapes! Oh, the agony! Did anyone see me? Did MOM see me? Oh no! GOD definitely saw me! In one weak moment of hunger, I was certain I was now destined for the fiery pits of no return. I did not like this feeling one bit. Terrified of what my parents would say or do to me, I held onto my deep, dark, treacherous secret. The "or else" was sure to come now! At bedtime, I fell to my knees and prayed God would forgive me. I subsequently refused to eat another grape for months in repentance. Please don't laugh at my confession because I am feeling my childhood shame all over again just on recall.

SINCERITY embodies many things, but most strongly it embodies values of honesty, integrity, humility, and truth. These are deep motivators for people like me. I'm not sure how many other people grew up in "or else" parenting culture. I have no statistics on how many have ever stolen a few grocery store grapes and agonized over it for months. But I do know that 12% of my survey respondents are strongly motivated by SINCERITY and specifically act in virtuous and positive ways because of it. They seek to connect, partner, and collaborate with others who share their deep value system, and they are tremendously turned off by people who do not.

I also know that SINCERITY, at only 12% of the working culture, may suggest people don't care about the virtues of SINCERITY. However, this statistic can be misleading, as most people underrate SINCERITY because they believe it should be a given. I liken it to when you order via the drive-thru of a fast-food restaurant. When you place your order, chances are that you rarely say, "and please include napkins." You assume the napkins are a given and are already in the bag. You overlook their importance until you need them—mid-drive when your fingers are dripping with fried chicken grease or ketchup is sliding off your burger onto your white shirt. Suddenly you feel indignant that there are no napkins, and your entire fast-food experience is potentially ruined. SINCERITY, like napkins, should always just be in the bag! We often don't value it until we discover how vitally we need it and don't have it.

We all know we live in a world filled with lies, half-truths, deception, and other less than sincere attributes. Yet we aspire to live in truth and goodness, free from the destructive snares deceitful practices get us into. Regardless of our human flaws and foibles, we ultimately value the higher and better living SINCERITY promotes. We want those same values in our workplaces, and we want our leaders to exemplify these values to show us the way. The consensus is that we expect "everyday people" to slip up from time to time, but most people offer little forgiveness for the leader who lacks SINCERITY. This feeling is especially true for people who identify with a strong SINCERITY S-Motivator.

If SINCERITY is your S-Motivator, you likely desire....

- ✓ Honesty from the people you work with and especially from your leaders
- ✓ The ability to be transparent, vulnerable, and authentic

- ✓ An organization that represents integrity with its employees and customers
- ✓ Humility and accountability when mistakes are made
- ✓ To be valued as trustworthy and treated fairly
- ✓ Open and truthful environments where actions speak louder than words
- ✓ A caring culture that respects diverse ideas and where it's safe to voice opinions
- ✓ Loyalty, commitment, and connection based on shared values of truth

If you are leading people with a strong SINCERITY S-Motivator, here is what they seek from you….

- ✓ To know they can trust you, no matter what
- ✓ To know they are trusted, no matter what
- ✓ Your commitment to leading a caring culture of accountability and truth
- ✓ Communication that is open, honest, empathic, and clear
- ✓ Freedom to speak openly and express differences constructively
- ✓ Consistent, authentic, and predictable behaviors that align with your words (Say = Do!)
- ✓ Respect, fairness, and consistency of rules, policies, and discipline
- ✓ Actions that demonstrate honesty, humility, fairness, empathy, kindness, and integrity

What Happens if You Don't Serve Up SINCERITY?

"I don't trust him."

"Something about her seems shady."

"This company isn't loyal to me so why should I be loyal to them?"

"We mislead our customers, and no one seems to care."

"I wish they'd just be honest."

Have you ever heard these or similar complaints? If so, you were most likely operating in a culture that lacked honesty and integrity overall, or you were hearing the grievances of a worker with a high SINCERITY S-

Motivator. If it was the latter, the passion and commitment that worker once brought to the workplace likely transformed into regular thoughts or even active plans for their personal exodus.

When your connection with others is not built upon a respected level of SINCERITY, distrust will grow and your ability to effectively lead will shrink. Trust is that non-negotiable trait most necessary for you and for your organization to function at its best. SINCERITY is both fundamental and emotional. Therefore, of all the S-Motivators, a lack of SINCERITY leads to the greatest long-term damages of a single relationship and of an entire organizational culture.

Consider this example. Envision a time when you felt cheated, treated poorly, or betrayed. Who do you see in your mind? When you think of that person who wronged you or the incident in question, how do your emotions feel or change? Perhaps the emotion caused a physical reaction. You sighed. Your heart rate sped up. Your eyes rolled or squinted. Your lip tightened. Depending on how hurtful or damaging the experience was, you may sense a little emotion, or you may feel a lot. Those are the feelings a lack of SINCERITY causes. Just as you can feel this negative energy personally, you can sense or feel this damage in your organization. Instead of being in a fun or engaging workplace, people are now in a place of conflict, tension, egg-shell walking, and behind-the-back talking. Eventually, these negative attributes overtake the workplace.

When someone doesn't know something (lacks SOLUTIONS), we may be disappointed or frustrated by their lack of knowledge or intellect, but we aren't emotionally hurt or damaged by it. However, when someone betrays our trust or is dishonest (lacks SINCERITY), we often feel this offense personally. Someone's dishonesty or insincerity can threaten our security, beliefs, and values. We instinctively go into self-protection mode, which changes the way we work, relate, and communicate, and not for the better. When you lead an insincere organization, dishonesty will be evident at almost every level. People cut corners in their work duties, tell half-truths in their reports or feedback, lack genuineness with customers, and lie to each other and to you. As a result, your products or services will fail to live up to the desired or intended quality or integrity. Dishonesty becomes the status quo. Here are a couple of glaring examples that immediately come to mind.

Case Study 1
"Ima Forger"

A temporary employee of two months, Ima Forger primarily worked in the mailroom. At only 24 years of age, she had so much to learn about the way the world of workplace conflict unfolds. She came to me to vent about a workplace incident that caused her a great deal of distress.

A payroll administrator abruptly resigned, which left the company with no one to sign off on paychecks. A senior supervisor asked Ima to forge the payroll administrator's signature so that paychecks could go out on time that week. Just a rookie, temporary employee, Ima did not know a lot about the company or their processes, but she did know she was being asked to do something dishonest and maybe illegal. What made this incident least palatable is that she was asked to forge a signature at a *law firm*!

Prior to this one request, Ima loved her job, and she had admiration and respect for the people who worked there. She had hopes of being signed on to a permanent position and possibly moving up the ranks into leadership herself. In one ill-advised incident that directly offended young Ima's integrity and morals, she greatly distrusted leadership and no longer felt comfortable working there. She thought about posting a blog on social media about the exploit she had been subjected to. Can you imagine the potential backlash for this law firm?

A leader who was thinking empathically could have prevented such a dishonest decision. No one with true SINCERITY would think to use a young person, or anyone for that matter, as a pawn to do the dirty deeds of an organization. Even if the supervisor's degree of integrity was poor, thinking empathically first would have caused them to consider the potential damage to the person being placed in such a compromising position, let alone the potential backlash to the company if the truth ever got out. The only good thing that came of this situation is the supervisor set an example for Ima of the leader she never wanted to be.

Case Study 2
"DaJuana Hurt"

I found DaJuana Hurt crying in a hallway after we concluded a day-long team building workshop. Our goal was to evaluate and help build trust in this department of administrative and analytics professionals. When I pulled DaJuana aside to inquire what was wrong, I was alarmed to find she had a deep belief and fear that her leadership was racist and had a long history of discrimination. She had gone so far as to keep a seven-year written account of the lack of eligible promotions of African Americans and Hispanics in the organization. After over a decade in her current position, without promotion although she had applied six different times, and in observance of other minorities being overlooked, she felt stuck. Understandably, she was hurt, angry, and insecure.

DaJuana said her organization always touted a commitment to fairness, diversity, and inclusion. When she confidentially voiced her concerns to her supervisor, whom she trusted, she later found out through a colleague with knowledge of senior management discussions that her boss leaked her concerns. Her boss also cast her as a complainer and a company cancer who was looking to stir up racial trouble. DaJuana believed if she could not trust her supervisor with her concerns, there was definitely no one else she could trust. She was fearful and tearful that her job was now in jeopardy after a decade of loyalty.

Six months later, I unexpectedly received an email from DaJuana telling me she was seeking to resign from the organization, but she was bitterly determined to take the agency down on her way. This was a sad outcome to such a preventable situation. Subsequently, the supervisor struggled to be seen as trustworthy, with her staff often walking on eggshells, and the agency had to invest a lot of money and time to repair the negative perceptions and employee turnover their lack of SINCERITY caused. Empathic leadership should be based on creating a mutual trust that fosters best intentions and prevents perceptions and feelings from ever rising to this degree of conflict.

Why SINCERITY Is So Important...

Let's start by considering the definition of SINCERITY. SINCERITY is the quality or state of being free from pretense, deceit, or hypocrisy. No founder or leadership team wants those qualities to define their culture or organization, yet these facets are human nature. Therefore, you must lead with a commitment to saying and doing the right things, the truthful things, and the best things for all involved. Otherwise, a negative culture overrun with conflict could become your leadership reality.

SINCERITY connects the dots of truth and integrity and must be baked into the fiber of who you are and what you bring to the workplace as a leader. You will never develop into your greatest version of leadership without SINCERITY. In fact, leaders and entire organizations have crumbled because they failed to tap into how important SINCERITY was to their workers. With SINCERITY operating as your guiding principle or core value, empathy becomes much easier to display and experience, because the relationships you build with others are authentic and caring. You have a greater desire and ability to build and maintain trust in those relationships and therefore can lead and motivate others to do their best work without the emotional and psychological limitations distrust creates.

Establishing true SINCERITY is also critical for understanding your own values, orientation, needs, and motivation. In other words, SINCERITY enables you to be true to yourself, which requires a healthy level of humility. You will be able to assess and embrace your own foibles and vulnerabilities, as well as strengths, and use that knowledge to effectively apply yourself with others in the workplace. When you operate with SINCERITY, you don't have to struggle with imposter syndrome or other feelings of being fake or inadequate. That's the power of self-knowledge and ultimately self-love. This is where confidence lies, and that confidence speaks volumes in your ability to lead others. Being true with others begins with being true with yourself, and your greatest achievements in life and leadership will be built upon this virtue of SINCERITY.

Case Study 3
"Mr. Goodman"

My son Andrew is driven by SINCERITY. While working in his first full-time job after college as a Customer Service/Technical Support Rep for a security alarm company, he experienced his first taste of the ideal empathic leader. Almost every day when I asked how his day went, Andrew oozed with excitement, laughter, and sometimes profound thought about something Mr. Goodman did or said. He frequently ended his statements with, "Mr. Goodman is a great leader, Mom. He is exactly the kind of good leader you always talk about in your speeches."

I asked Andrew to tell me what made Mr. Goodman so "good." I wanted him to paint a clear picture, and his ability to trust his supervisor's sincerity was most evident: "Mr. Goodman has a way of treating every person as though he really cares about you—not just as an employee, but as a person. Even though working customer service can feel like a frustrating and monotonous job, just answering phones and listening to complaints all day, he says things that make you feel significant. He helps you stay focused and have empathy for the customer as a person, and he helps me to remember I am only human, too. I don't know, **I guess I just really trust him.** He doesn't just tell me what I'm doing wrong; he shows me how to do things better. I have top scores as a Customer Service Rep again this month because of him. He helps me to not get frustrated. He always follows up when he monitors one of my calls and asks me about how I was feeling or what I was thinking. He doesn't sugar coat things, but he tells you the truth, both good and bad. He's just exactly the kind of leader I hope to be one day. I'm learning a lot from him."

Who doesn't want to be THAT leader? I felt like I knew Mr. Goodman, because I've talked about this type of sincere leadership for a long time. It meant a lot to me that my son, who has been listening to me lecture for years, had an opportunity to know this type of leadership was attainable. It meant even more to know he was driven to attain this level of leadership for himself. I'm grateful Mr. Goodman "walked my talk" and set the example for an emerging group of Gen Z leaders like my son.

Case Study 4
"Phil Heard"

My own example of SINCERITY is personal. During one of the absolute lowest moments of my career, after my son was diagnosed with a brain tumor, I spent almost nine months unemployed, living off credit cards, trying to get him to a place of health and stability. I desperately needed gainful employment and was offered a job by Phil Heard at a large Fortune 500 mortgage company. Phil learned of my plight through a casual conversation and demonstrated unparalleled empathy and trust in offering me a job even though I had very little mortgage experience. His ability to extend so much sincere trust to me at such a vulnerable time made it easy for me to immediately trust him right back.

I can list on one hand the number of leaders I've met that I'd run through walls for. Phil gets the index finger of my count. He led by example, not in a way that he always did everything right. He led by the example of being sincere in his caring character, choices, and communication. When I did something incorrectly or fell behind, he was quick to pull me into his office, offer me a motivating pep talk, and explain my errors. Additionally, he did something unusual: he immediately assigned me a mentor, explaining the partnership would be beneficial for both of us.

Phil paired me up with Kevin, an introverted facts and figures sales dynamo who needed to learn to "loosen up" and gain empathic leadership skills. Apparently, Phil felt dealing with an outgoing, communicative, African American, single mom like me might open up a relatively dormant side of Kevin. Conversely, I needed to learn the more technical and detailed ins and outs of mortgage processing. We were as opposite as opposites can get. We had very different people styles, culture backgrounds, and personalities, and I truly believe we would have never spoken more than a casual hello to one another had it not been for Phil's decision.

Kevin and I did not necessarily trust each other at first, but we shared a deep trust in Phil, who cared enough about our individual weaknesses to partner us and grow us because of our strengths. My sales took off the following month, and my mentor was not only promoted to leadership, but even dared to step onto the dance floor at the company Christmas party! Empathic leaders who sincerely care about growing their people accomplish amazing things!

To empathically lead with SINCERITY means you must understand that each person has a varying degree of ability to trust others. High Trusters trust easily but are tremendously disappointed when trust is broken, and they may take a long time to recover, if ever. Low Trusters rarely trust, especially in new relationships. They have typically been burned in the past and require extra layers of SECURITY in their work relationships in order to perform at their best. Moderate Trusters meet you at the 50-yard line and watch you carefully. You are either scoring SINCERITY points or losing them, all based on your words and actions. In all cases, trust must be earned. Care enough about people and the relationships you are forging to learn where trust resides.

Remember that you will always have a select few people in your organization with high levels of integrity (call them the self-policed grape stealers) who hold values like honesty, fairness, and respect in highest regard. While some people can and will cut corners, fudge a number or two, or cast a Cheshire Cat grin while they pull the wool over a customer's eyes, those who value SINCERITY operate with a strict moral compass and cannot remain for very long in places where the values of SINCERITY are not present. For them, it's too emotionally taxing or stressful to do so. These people are rare gems. Fight to keep them. They want to look up to you and run through proverbial walls for you. Once they know mutual SINCERITY exists, don't be surprised when they do!

As my son Andrew learned, SINCERITY includes sharing the hard truths, and thus you must recognize every conversation will not be a comfortable one. Have the courage to say and do the right things in the face of adversity, and realize most people will respect and trust you even greater when you do. These days, one of the hardest things to be is *honest*. But respect grows immeasurably when words match deeds, especially in challenging situations. **SINCERITY begins with being true to yourself**, so you must be clear about your own values and recognize when you have a value conflict with others. Act wisely and swiftly to keep distrust from growing and spreading. Grow your conflict resolution skills and learn how to have the "tough conversations" that maintain mutual respect instead of fostering dishonesty. Always keep in mind, **the real opponent is DISTRUST!** So, listen empathically, speak truthfully, lead sincerely.

Wrapping Up SINCERITY

Here is the empathetic thought I want you to keep closest to your chest. **We tend to underestimate the value of SINCERITY until we have been the ones harmed by lack thereof.** While we like to think SINCERITY is a given in relationships and in the workplace, it simply is not. You need to intentionally prioritize SINCERITY to bring out the best in all, and you start by being self-aware of your own values, and then being aware of how those values align with others. In the words of Social Styles pioneers Dr. David Merrill and Roger Reed:

> *"It's vital to understand your own behavior and how it affects others. To others, you are what you say and do—no more, no less. Most people do not know—cannot know— your motives or your inner thoughts. They can, however, hear and see what you say and do."*

You communicate SINCERITY best when your intentions are humble, pure, and clear, and when your words and actions align. Communicate with SINCERITY and deliver leadership that reflects it in all you do. Empathy not only helps you collaborate with others who desire connection and workplaces based on integrity, but it also helps you understand the human flaws and struggles that cause people to lack trust, honesty, and SINCERITY. Empathy helps you display wisdom in the way you approach discipline and correction, and in offering the grace needed to improve and strengthen relationships, culture, and productivity. There will be no need for "sour grapes" (or stolen ones) if you prioritize SINCERITY in your leadership and show genuine respect and appreciation for those motivated by it in your organization.

SINCERITY AAA Exercises

Awareness

1) Self-assess your level of "Trust-Ability." Are you a High, Moderate, or Low Truster? Why do you think you trust the way you do?

2) Rate (1 -10) yourself on how trustworthy and sincere you believe others perceive you to be. Write down why you rate yourself this way.

3) Rate how well you trust others on your team or in your organization. Write down the reasons you do or do not trust. Do these people know how you feel and why you feel the way you do?

4) Here are the four areas where I find leaders need the most self-awareness work in communicating or demonstrating SINCERITY. Self-assess the following:

- **Intentions:** What are they? Does everyone know? Are you communicating with clarity and following up on promises? Do your intentions represent honest, fair, and inclusive ideals? Do your actions match your words? In what ways?

- **Feedback:** Are you appreciative? How do you show it? Do you regularly offer praise? To whom and in what ways? How do you approach conflict conversations? Are you passive or avoidant? Or are you prone to be too harsh or critical? How do you know? Do you dread evaluation meetings or welcome them? How often do you have these meetings?

- **Gossip**: Do you participate? If not, do you shut down unproven rumors when others gossip?

- **Apologizing:** Is it hard for you to say "I'm sorry" or admit when you have made a mistake? Are you gracious when others apologize or make a mistake?

Accountability

This month, survey the people you work with. If you are comfortable, and have established a high degree of cultural trust, ask your team to answer the same questions above, and then ask them to answer the same questions about you. Openly discuss the answers and ways to keep each other accountable to grow in SINCERITY together.

If you are new to growing trust with your team, or just desire a higher opportunity for honest feedback, survey anonymously or call in a third-party consultant to administer SINCERITY-oriented team building and communication exercises. Be sure to include Empathic or Active Listening sessions.

Action

Once you have discussed ways to grow in SINCERITY with your team, follow up regularly. Remember, people often take SINCERITY for granted (just like the napkins!). One small unresolved conflict is all it takes for distrust to permeate and precipitate in your relationships and culture. Plan with your team how to best manage conflicts should they arise. Regularly encourage opportunities to discuss any challenges and ways to be more empathetic with each other.

CHAPTER 9

SELFLESSNESS

The grocery store's strategy was set. Every employee knew the mission. The win was in sight. The helpful stock representative greeted customers as they visited each aisle and took careful inventory of the shelves. The cashiers communicated, smiled, and connected with their customers while ringing up the items. The clerk efficiently bagged the items and placed them in the carts. And Ricky's job was to scream "I GOT IT" while enthusiastically maneuvering the cart out of the store to the respective shopper's vehicle. The end game: a memorable shopping experience for another satisfied (and perhaps slightly startled) customer. Can you see it? Can you feel it?

How cool is it to labor in an environment where you know you are working purposefully with others towards something bigger than yourself? How motivating is it to engage with others who genuinely care about winning together? How awesome is it to thrive in a culture where individuals and their unique gifts are valued, no matter how different or extreme, because everyone has the ability and autonomy to contribute in a special way? While celebrating and appreciating individuals is vital, winning *together* is the ultimate prize. This is what I love so much about team sports, and what I relish about Ricky's story. Connection. Communication. Camaraderie. Collaboration. That's SELFLESSNESS!

I started playing team sports when I was eight years old. My first experience was on the T-ball team for the Silver Hill Boy's and Girl's Club in Marlow Heights, Maryland. A year later, I discovered basketball and was hooked. That sport quickly became my love and later my ticket to college, to coaching collegiate sports, and to broadcasting college and professional basketball for over thirty years. On every team I joined, I learned so much about who I was and how my individual skills and character traits contributed to the team. Each year I played, I gained confidence and a sense of connection and family. I learned that there was no room for selfishness if you wanted your team to win. To this day, my college teammates and I still get together at least once a year to laugh, tell old stories, and catch up on each other's lives. We still help each other win in whatever personal or professional ways we can. Go 'Cuse Sisters!

For years after my son's brain tumor surgery and subsequent visual impairment, he struggled to fit into his peer social circles. He was bullied, ostracized, and depressed. I prayed he would be able to find camaraderie through participating in sports, or belonging to any type of team environment, because I knew the value of teamwork. I also experienced the maturation and positive character benefits that resulted from being a good teammate. When he was 15, Drew came home one day and told me he made the goalball team at the Florida School for the Deaf and Blind. I was thrilled! I think I even let out a little proud-Mommy cry. Fortunately, he had a coach he greatly admired, which made the experience all the better. At the time, Drew was a relatively awkward, insecure, introverted, only child. I knew this was the opportunity that could help him find his "I GOT IT," feel the pride and joy of winning, and develop the grit and perseverance needed to bounce back from losing. And it was!

Over the past year of my research, I have witnessed a surge in the number of poll participants who selected SELFLESSNESS as their core S-Motivator. In fact, the percentage of respondents jumped from 13% in 2022 to 26% in 2023. I found this sudden spike interesting, especially since we were coming out of a pandemic where one of the biggest losses to human beings was social connection. Apparently, people now more deeply desire to be with, support, and be supported by others with common objectives. I've also discovered that SELFLESSNESS ranks high among the Gen Z generation, team sport athletes, and corporate workers with leaders who emphasize and prioritize a strong team culture. Some people naturally gravitate towards collaborating with others to accomplish goals, while others are coached into it. I've also noticed many SELFLESSNESS motivated people are often described as humble, genuine, giving, helpful, kind, amiable, or fun, and they look for these traits in others. They truly believe and epitomize TEAM (Together Everyone Achieves More).

If SELFLESSNESS is your S-Motivator, you most likely desire....

- ✓ The energy and loyalty of a team or family environment
- ✓ Helping others genuinely and humbly
- ✓ Being committed to something bigger than yourself, going above and beyond
- ✓ To know you belong and others have your back
- ✓ Being motivated and inspired for a challenging but achievable team win
- ✓ An undeniable spirit of enjoyment, togetherness, or unity
- ✓ True culture of diversity, equity, inclusion, and belongingness
- ✓ A job well done where everyone feels included and valued

If you are leading people with a strong SELFLESSNESS S-Motivator, this is what they seek from you:

- ✓ The prioritization of TEAM with your demonstration and reinforcement by example
- ✓ Constant communication of unity, fun, and "we win this together!"
- ✓ Opportunities for collaboration, team building, and purposeful assistance
- ✓ Genuineness and humility in what you say and do
- ✓ Big picture communication and goals with clearly defined roles, tasks, and contributions
- ✓ A helpful, empathic, encouraging, coaching style of leadership

- ✓ Clearly defined, believable, and achievable "wins"
- ✓ Your personal commitment to diversity, equity, inclusion, and belonging

What Happens if You Don't Serve Up SELFLESSNESS?

I have a favorite quote pertaining to selfish or arrogant people:

> ***If you think it's all about you, soon you will be right, because "YOU" is all you will have!***

I could sum up this entire section in that quote alone, so please re-read it. However, because I, too, passionately value SELFLESSNESS, I will go above and beyond to give you more context. Maybe you have experienced or have heard about teams or organizations where it feels like no one cares about each other, and leadership takes the biggest hit of the complaint. Cliques, silos, blaming, in-fighting for favoritism or position, and poor morale are the most obvious tangibles in a culture not driven by an empathic and selfless leader. People who enjoy spreading positivity and helping others often feel awkward and lost in environments where no true opportunity or encouragement to engage in this way exists.

SELFLESSNESS and SINCERITY share commonalities in that they are acutely people-driven motivators with trust as an anchor of performance. Trust grows in a culture where people driven by SELFLESSNESS feel they are depended on to make positive contributions towards a common goal and towards the humanity of helping others. Respectively, distrust grows when there is no encouragement or opportunity to do so. Realize that helping others is a genuine and humble value for this selfless niche. When genuineness and humility are absent, poor morale and a lack of drive, direction, and purpose are the results. And while praise and appreciation are always welcome, those driven by SELFLESSNESS often prefer quiet recognition or team recognition so as not to appear arrogant or selfish. SELFLESSNESS S-Motivated people can often withdraw when they feel too much attention focused on individualism rather than group or team successes.

Regardless of what the vocational or project goal is, SELFLESSNESS-driven people see "making the team assist" as the ultimate end game. Therefore, leaders must help their SELFLESSNESS-driven people see how they matter (similar to their SIGNIFICANCE-driven counterparts). The difference is that they need to see how they matter as part of the big team picture—a part of something bigger than themselves—rather than their individual contributions. Without this connection, work isn't fun for them. As a result, the silo-effect of people looking for their tribe, deeply seeking where they fit in, and often complaining about when they don't kicks in. If you are not delivering this direction as a leader, your SELFLESSNESS-driven people will determine you are a "bad coach" and you may experience the pain of lonely, disconnected employees or cliques that are difficult to dismantle. Finally, if you are a leader who uses "I" more than "we," your lack of humility will quickly gather a lack of respect from your SELFLESSNESS-motivated kindred.

Case Study 1
"Don Fitten"

For as long as Don could remember, people described him as a genius or a geek. He didn't mind being "the smart one" everyone counted on to solve complex problems, but he did not like the negative connotation of being the proverbial "know it all." His supervisor didn't help his reputation, as he constantly compared everyone else to a "Don standard" which Don found humiliating. Don had a big SELFLESSNESS S-Motivator. Had his supervisor ever empathically taken the time to get to know Don for who he truly was (or if Don had learned to speak up for himself), his supervisor would have recognized Don's psychological need for humility.

Overall, Don was shy and socially awkward. As a kid, he got picked on in school for being a nerd. Over time, however, he found that with the right set of lively peers who accepted his giftedness, he could come out of his shell. With his high intellect came a great sense of humor that he reserved for the people he trusted and who accepted him. Don always deeply desired to have fun and fit in with others. However, he often lacked confidence that he could or would. As an adult, he was just a big kid who enjoyed the feeling of creating, communicating, and collaborating with and for others. If he felt rejected, or conversely, if he felt overly praised in any way, he would emotionally retreat. While he wanted to be recognized for his knowledge or good work, he also wanted to belong. The limelight was never his end game.

Don sensed that his supervisor's constant compliments and comparisons were making his peers jealous and annoyed. As result, Don was less motivated to speak up in meetings, which subtly hindered the team's productivity. When the Covid-19 pandemic forced everyone into a remote environment, Don struggled with a greater feeling of isolation, disconnection, and drive. Zoom meetings with cameras off and a supervisor who failed to create a culture that highlighted team accomplishments became more prevalent and discontenting than ever. Don sought career coaching as he failed to feel motivated or connected, and he was exploring other employment possibilities.

Case Study 2
"Ida Best"

Renee admitted she was nervous when she sought me for career coaching. She never engaged in coaching before, but since her company was providing the resource as an added benefit, she was eager to give it a try. Renee realized she was such a SELFLESSNESS-driven person that it felt a bit strange seeking help for herself. By mid-conversation, I recognized she still wasn't seeking help for just herself, but for her coworkers too. She needed conflict resolution strategies to deal with her boss, Ida Best.

Prior to Ida's hiring to oversee the marketing department, Renee was the Project Manager for a large annual event her corporation had sponsored for the past five years. Renee was proud to lead such a fun and collaborative effort and team. Many of the workers volunteered additional time to the project to ensure it was a success, including Renee. Anyone involved in this initiative knew they would be working long hours on a dedicated team of selfless contributors. This year, during the first senior leaders' meeting, Renee became disgruntled as she listened to Ida give an update and take full responsibility for the progress and success of the program Renee was overseeing. Ida never mentioned Renee or any of the various volunteers by name. Instead, she said things like, "I am overseeing this," and "I am making sure of that." It was as if Ida was running the entire initiative by herself, yet she had never even attended a single meeting!

Renee wanted advice on how to initiate a conversation with Ida to help her understand how the cohort had always operated as a team, sharing the praise as much as they shared the workload, and how offensive it was to many of the volunteers that Ida appeared to be a pompous, limelight abuser. What was interesting in this case was that Renee struggled with speaking up because she wanted to be sure she did so in a way that Ida would not think she was jealous or desired the credit for herself. Renee wanted to use the right words and phrasing to advise Ida that the team concept and culture is what kept these volunteers so actively engaged and desiring to go above and beyond. She ultimately wanted Ida to present herself as humble and more respectful in the future.

Why SELFLESSNESS is So Important

SELFLESSNESS represents the best of who we are, not just as individuals, but collectively, as a group, an organization, a team, a family, a human race. Some people have to be coaxed into this unselfish mindset, while others come by it quite naturally. Many of us feel a humility of spirit that invites us all to play nice together and to be supportive at work and beyond. This spirit encourages. It complements and compliments. It craves an opportunity to help and be accepted, respected, and needed, never failing to offer the same. SELFLESSNESS is the critical and complete vision of what a true empathic leader can do to help each member of the team know they are playing this game of life to win—and that win is one of acceptance and connection through service to one another.

As a child growing up in the Baptist church, I often marveled at the alter call. I am a Christian, and while I did not fully understand what that meant as a ten-year-old, I knew it was something special, like being on a team. At alter call, parishioners cheered, and many times cried as others came to the front of the church to accept the gift of Christ's saving grace and dedicate their lives to God. I often heard my grandmother cry out, "Hallelujah, another one made it over!" Everyone in church celebrated at this spiritual party that I didn't quite understand, but I still felt invited to. Even at that young age, I knew I was witnessing tremendous SELFLESSNESS. Grandma was genuinely happy, to the point of joyful tears, that another human being—a complete stranger—came forward to be unified with a family of believers who purposed to follow God's plan to live in love, peace, purpose, and prosperity for humanity.

It may sound cliché, but it is true: no person is an island. We all need someone in some shape or fashion. Knowing that we cannot exist on Earth without other human beings working together towards a common good makes SELFLESSNESS fundamental. But realize that not all things fundamental translate as functional. In a world of social media likes and followers, political agendas, and money matters, we have arguably fallen into a "me-first" culture. Therefore, leaders must be intentional about encouraging acts of selfless service, a team-first mentality, and practicality. The good news is cultures are more likely to follow their leaders when they know their leaders are willing to place the needs of others above their own. Directing most every unselfish team is a selfless leader demonstrating by example. Here is some more good news: acts of SELFLESSNESS are highly observable, benefiting both givers and receivers, so it is one of the easiest ways for leaders to find the empathy and example needed to make an impact.

Case Study 3
"Manny Hatts"

I sat at the restaurant patiently waiting for my meal. This was unusual, since displaying patience with anything, especially when I'm hungry, is indeed a rarity! Even more peculiar was that the middle-aged gentleman who was my server this evening was also the restaurant manager. "Did someone get sick? Were they short staffed?" I had to ask. The answer surprised me and left an impression on my future thoughts on selfless leadership by example. This manager informed me that he was adamant everyone should help out as it pertained to the customer wherever they could. They operated as a team, and no job was too menial or tedious for anyone to do, including managers.

Dining at this restaurant was a joy. The manager and every server on the floor was perky, friendly, energetic, and eager to run back and forth from the kitchen to their various tables to serve customers. They laughed with each other, and I heard quick conversations like, "What do you need? I'll grab it." The energy was incomparable. No wonder I hadn't become impatient waiting for my food! I was confident this organization had a leader who ignited this impeccable teamwork with his empathic example! It's difficult to complain how hard your job is or how no one understands or cares when you have a motivated and motivating manager doing the same work with great enthusiasm.

For some business models, it may seem too confusing or upsetting for different levels of the organizational hierarchy to wear interchangeable hats. Traditional organizational engineers are sure to find flaws in this structure. But this restaurant mastered any structure challenges with well-intentioned and well-designed SELFLESSNESS. I'm sure each person still had some specific and independent roles and responsibilities to carry out, but they found a shared responsibility in directly serving their customers. No back office bosses here! No power or ego trips! Just great customer service through acts of SELFLESSNESS. I'm a witness. When selfless teamwork is at its best it leaves everyone hungry for more!

Case Study 4
"E.Z. Dusset"

E.Z. Dusset was new on the job. He was also new to social work, so he did not yet understand the demands of being a case worker for this non-profit organization serving the homeless population in Jacksonville, FL. He didn't yet understand all the rules. To his chagrin, he got called into his supervisor's office for breaking one of those rules. However, chagrin turned to annoyance once his manager shared what he MUST do moving forward: take a 15-minute walk. "Surely, she must be kidding! If I'm running behind on my caseloads, I'm wasting time I could be using to get work done!" he scoffed. But the rule was written and clear. It was also purposeful, as E.Z. would soon discover.

Every employee was required to take two 15-minute breaks (preferably a walk) plus a lunch break. Moreover, the breaks had to be taken away from their desk, and employees were not allowed to do anything work related while on breaks. Over the years, leadership saw how emotionally taxing the case worker's position could be. The holistic well-being of their workers was so paramount that it became a written rule. It wasn't until E.Z. had his first tough case, only two weeks into the job, that he realized how impactful this mandate truly was. He had to be the bearer of bad news to a young, single mother of two toddlers regarding her housing assistance expiration. It was far more emotional than he imagined.

During E.Z.'s 15-minute walk to clear his heart and head, he realized how much respect and gratitude he had for his leadership team. Not only was caring for a homeless population deeply in need of help a selfless job, but the organization had many SELFLESSNESS S-Motivated workers doing this tough work. This leadership team knew that the incidence of stress and burnout was high among people who are deeply motivated by SELFLESSNESS, because they tend to give so much, often at the expense of their own mental and emotional wellness. E.Z. quickly understood that it took empathy for his leaders to embrace this perspective and to care enough to put purposeful and compassionate rules in place to protect their team.

To empathically lead with SELFLESSNESS means you must be willing to be compassionate, sensitive, and understanding of people's individual needs. You must also make decisions on what is best for the greater good and needs of the team. At times, these two facets will seem at odds, as what is good for one may not be good for all, and vice versa. This is when your words and actions must clearly communicate an intention of acceptance and inclusiveness so respect for your leadership will override individual selfish desires or needs. If your team perceives you are always putting the team's needs first and displaying a genuine humility of spirit, they will follow that example. A culture that keeps everyone accountable to SELFLESSNESS is the ideal culture to build and work in.

When people feel their leaders are disingenuous, dissention among the ranks will become evident. Therefore, you must avoid perceptions of favoritism as well as bias, even though it is human nature to be subject to both. You also must maintain the self-awareness of your own selfish or seemingly arrogant behavior, as these are equally damaging to creating the teamwork culture you desire. Delegate fairly and remember to lead and to serve in some capacity. That is, after all, why we are all here. Every single one of us. I discovered "it's only about you long enough for you to discover it was never really about you." You come into your true leadership gift and potential once you embrace this concept. Leadership absolutely MUST be selfless. Many think it is about POWER. While it is true many leaders possess great power, with the selfish use of that power, failure will prove inevitable.

Over the past few years, I have discovered that the Gen Z population craves specific things from their leaders and their world. At the forefront is diversity, equity, inclusion, and belonging. Gone are the days where "diversity" was simply about a tangible metric based on ethnic, gender, or religious quotas. Gen Z has made it clear that they prefer workplace environments that tap into how they *feel* about all those things, plus their ideas, experiences, and cultural nuances. A perfect example of this happened to me personally. While teaching a public speaking class at the University of North Florida, I discovered that anime, which is a Japanese film and television animation, is not only a popular cultural art, but also a cherished one among my students. They seemed emotionally injured and disappointed that I dismissed its relative importance by quipping, "You all are into some new and different stuff, and I just don't get it. What ever happened to good old Bugs Bunny?" As the leader, they believe it is my job to get it, to understand it, and to appreciate and celebrate that it is important to *them*, even if I have no clue what it is all about.

Inclusion taps into whether they feel they are included. Are their thoughts and ideas welcomed? Are they deemed relevant to the conversation? Are they encouraged and offered opportunities for expression of their differences? Equity attempts to discover the ways people feel fairness is experienced. Gen Zers want to be assured they are receiving fair pay and career development opportunities and that this fairness is seen across the board, not solely based on their youth or inexperience. They believe that if all are participating, then all should receive fair compensation and provisions. Belonging is based on whether people feel like they fit in, despite the ways they may be perceived as different from a certain majority. Neurodiversity is a product of their generational upbringing, so concern for mental illness as well as provisions for mental wellness are an expectation of corporate culture. They may be quicker to discuss their mental health issues with an expectation you understand and empathize. Persons with disabilities, people who identify differently in terms of gender, sex, preferences, or orientation, or anyone once designated as being "different than the traditional norm," must be accepted and valued as the norm. For Gen Z, everyone belongs and has a right to feel they are psychologically safe, respected, valued, and provided for.

In short, SELFLESSNESS is about emotions and how people not only think, but also how they feel they are part of the team. Thus, today's leader must prove they are driven by empathy and emotional intelligence to understand these feelings and to care enough to courageously act and make decisions accordingly.

Wrapping Up SELFLESSNESS

I began with the end in mind for this chapter, and I meant what I said, so, it bears repeating, **"If you think it's all about you, soon you will be right, because YOU is all you will have."** Just as it takes a village to raise a strong family, it takes an equally strong village to create a workplace family. Sharing is caring! Diverse ideas, gifts, talents, skills, knowledge, curiosity, creativity, and innovation must all feel welcomed, embraced, and respected, even when you think you are the smartest or most capable person in the room. Leading with SELFLESSNESS means people are free and encouraged to share what they know or have to make the culture better without intimidation, envy, or over-concern for individual credit. The leader may be responsible for creating and encouraging a culture of SELFLESSNESS, but it only takes root when the leaders are consistently involving and crediting the team for the company's success and livelihood.

For truly empathic leaders, SELFLESSNESS is the vision and the end game. SELFLESSNESS naturally lives and breathes more strongly in some and may need a little help developing in others. Either way, you can believe your team will embrace teamwork as you do. You are always the example, not the exception. Please also remember that you will not always get everything right, and even the best teams occasionally fail. But having a mindset and mission of SELFLESSNESS will certainly improve your chances of success. Regardless of what setbacks may arise, you will know the thrill and support of overcoming and winning as a team. For SELFLESSNESS-driven people, that makes any challenge worth facing, and any game worth playing, and any team (and leader) worth playing for!

SELFLESSNESS AAA Exercises

Awareness

Visualize the team and culture you want to have. Then, answer the following questions. Be specific and include examples.

- What core values do you want your team to represent?

- How will you serve your customers?

- How will you treat each other?

- What communication is needed and valued?

- How do you as the leader empower each individual with greatness so that the collective team ultimately exceeds expectations?

- How can each member have a voice, even if they don't always get a vote?

- What collaborative processes can be improved?

- What individual efforts can become more collaborative?

Accountability

With your team, write down that ideal team picture and perform a gap analysis to identify areas of improvement. Ask for additional feedback on what the team would most desire to include, or what new team-oriented ideas you can implement to enhance process, productivity, or performance.

Action

- Plan a Team Building or Culture Building Session with your team using an outside consulting firm no more than three months out. (Procrastinating such events is very common so give yourself a real date and deadlines.) Plan to address some of the questions above, paying close attention to the areas of improvement. Create excitement around the opportunity to grow together and to do something family/team-oriented and fun.

- If your resources and time allow, commit to a team or company retreat, preferably away from the office and at an interesting or adventurous venue or location.

- If you wish to do something smaller or more cost efficient, identify online resources to conduct team building sessions yourself, or seek assistance from your HR department if available. Also consider remote team building activities via Zoom or other virtual tools.

- If it is team culture you desire, engaging in fun activities that promote a culture of unity, service, and SELFLESSNESS is one of the best ways to help build it.

- Remember the importance of the emotional element inherent in great teams and great unity. Feeling connected is the goal, not simply talking about it. Make teamwork a reality!

CHAPTER 10

DEVELOPING YOUR LEADERSHIP 6-S

> *"Today a reader; tomorrow a leader."*
> *–Margaret Fuller*

For one last time, envision Ricky—a young man in his early twenties with thick, dark rimmed glasses, fair skin, brown hair, and medium height with a slightly hefty frame. His soft eyes drooped a little and his mouth hung open, slightly slanted to one side. He wore black orthopedic shoes that helped him stay balanced as he lifted his legs a bit clumsily to race through the store, looking for the next available customer with a loaded shopping cart. Oh yes, and he had an incredible set of lungs and vocal cords! Most of all, he was happy, energetic, enthusiastic, engaged, and engaging. His essence was infectious and heartwarming.

Now, as a graphic artist might do, transfer an image of your head and face onto the picture of Ricky you just imagined. But don't just see it—feel it. Feel the joy, the energy, and the enthusiasm Ricky displayed. Feel the support of the leadership team. Feel the empowerment of working in a place where you feel SIGNIFICANCE, SECURITY, SOLUTIONS, STRUCTURE, SINCERITY, and SELFLESSNESS. I want you to experience empathy through the Ricky persona, much as I did. I don't want you to imagine what it might feel like to be cognitively disabled. I want you to imagine what it's like to experience the excitement and the pride of feeling purposeful, despite any obstacles you might face. Really feel it! That's the feeling that can motivate your team to greatness.

We sometimes look at people who are differently abled as being, well, different. But aren't we all different in one way or another? Those differences make us unique. We all just want to matter, to belong, and to be respected and accepted. We all also feel fearful and anxious at times, especially when trying something new or challenging. Feel that nerve-racking interview or presentation. Feel that first day on the job. Feel that first time you failed or cost the company a setback. Feel the frustration and hurt of being judged or limited by others. That's all empathy really is. It's getting into the other person's shoes and being sensitive to when the fit isn't right. It's being excited when the fit feels great and running alongside him or her, jumping for joy while screaming, "I GOT IT!"

Ricky's Empathic Leader in All of Us

When you are willing to take the time to understand or deeply feel another's perspective or experience, you are building leadership greatness. Ricky's story stuck with me so intimately because as a single mother to a son with disabilities, I relate to what is required to help someone who has been "fouled," emotionally and physically, overcome and achieve. I had to give tremendous attention to his specific needs—needs I may not otherwise have been attentive to because I did not experience the same needs. I learned to tune in to his needs and motivations, which made me a wiser and a stronger leader and motivator overall.

Simulating my son's experience by asking questions and empathically listening so that I could "get into his shoes" was always the key to breakthrough moments of growth and productivity. Being as compassionate as I was courageous was also key. I didn't always get it right, however. Had you interviewed my son at the time, he may have said I never did! I sometimes had to make an unpopular judgment call when I thought I knew what was best because, after all, I was Supermom. I was the leader. But that decision was destined to fail when I reacted impulsively or simply relied on my knowledge or experiences without wholly considering his perspective and feelings.

Ricky's leaders had to compassionately understand Ricky's orientation, needs, and motivation to lead carefully and courageously. How unwise it would have been to assume he could or would be motivated to do everything the exact same way those who were not cognitively disabled did. In fact, it's unwise to assume anyone you work with shares the exact orientation, needs, experiences, feelings, or motivations, and expect maximum productivity and success. Ricky's supervisor tapped into the excitement and motivation Ricky felt when pushing the carts. You must employ the emotionally intelligent strategy of perspective-taking to understand the orientation, needs, and motivations of each of your staff or team members to achieve the leadership excellence you desire, and the leadership empathy your people need.

Baseline, Basics, and Best

When you or your hiring department bring in a new employee, you likely have already considered their baseline. You typically gather this information in the application, resume, and interview processes. You understand the employee's background, knowledge, skillsets, and experiences. You also have a generalized understanding of their basic needs—those things we all have in common, such as our physiological needs like food, shelter, and access to medical resources. We give people a job and benefits to satisfy those basic needs. The one thing I rarely hear interviewers tap into in the initial stages of hiring is the one answer leaders need to drive people to be their best. Personality assessments are admirable evaluators of orientation, but still may not always answer the critical question of motivation: *What drives or motivates you to do your best work?* The following image demonstrates the difference between orientation, needs, and motivation.

ORIENTATION, NEEDS, AND MOTIVATION
ORIENTATION
WHO ARE YOU? (BASELINE)
TRAITS
CHARACTER
VALUES
SKILLSET
MINDSET
KNOWLEDGE
EXPERIENCES
SPIRITUALITY
CULTURE
BACKGROUND
NEEDS
WHAT DO YOU NEED? (BASICS)
*PHYSIOLOGICAL:
AIR
FOOD
WATER
SLEEP
SHELTER
CLOTHING
*FINANCIAL/JOB
*RESOURCES
*PHYSICAL HEALTH
*MENTAL HEALTH
MOTIVATION
WHAT DRIVES YOU? (BEST)
PROBLEM SOLVING
ACHIEVEMENT
SELF-ACTUALIZATION
CONNECTION
SERVICE
PURPOSE
REWARDS
WINNING
ESTEEM
ORGANIZATION
LOYALTY
LEAD BEYOND JUST KNOWING THEIR BASELINE AND PROVIDING THEIR BASICS TO DRIVING THEM TO THEIR BEST!

Asking people what motivates them is so important because the question itself is empathic. It says, "I care about helping you achieve your best." You display true empathy when you make practical application of their answer in those times when life challenges make it difficult for that person to find the motivation to achieve on their own. Knowing their motivation is a way for you to communicate, "I understand what you need to get going and I care about your well-being and desire to be your best." It builds connection, trust, and ultimately loyalty, too.

When I was a sophomore on the Syracuse University Women's Basketball team in the mid- to late-1980s, a Jheri Curl was a popular, stylish hairstyle instead of a comical wig you might wear to an 80s party or see on a meme today. One day during practice, while performing running drills we called "200s," my drippy Jheri Curl and I had endured enough physical exertion. We could stand it no more! Gasping for air, drenched with sweat, and on fatigue overload, I passed out on the indoor track where we were conducting our conditioning drills. I had never felt so overwhelmingly and torturously exhausted in my entire 19 years of life. I checked out of that gym, and possibly out of life.

As I lay on the ground, I heard one coach yell, "Get up, Vera! Push yourself! You're better than this!" She was attempting to shame me at worst, appeal to my sense of pride at best. Both shame and pride formed a coup with exhaustion, overthrowing all my body parts in a complete revolt against movement and signs of life. But then something almost magical happened. In the distance, I heard one of my other coaches yell, "Come on, Vera! Get up! We *need* you! Who is going to be our shooter in Wednesday's game? We are counting on you to win!" Same moment of exhaustion. Same mental and physical circumstances. Different communication. When I heard the second coach, I was motivated to get up. She empathically appealed to my sense of SIGNIFICANCE and SELFLESSNESS. Even though I was in complete defiance due to fatigue, she helped me see how I mattered and how the team needed me to use my skillset to help us win. Miraculously, I got up off that track with renewed energy and drive to complete my running drills.

Empathy truly is a superpower! Once you develop the knowledge and skillset to use empathy by tapping into others' motivations, you, too, will be able to help drive people beyond baseline and basics to their best. The second coach knew the right words to use to drive me from a place of complete exhaustion to that of going above and beyond to perform, to produce, and to passionately play my position, even in the face of great adversity. This is what learning S-Motivators is all about. Your growth in empathic listening, communicating, and ultimately applying the knowledge you gain about each individual will be that superpower that motivates them to be their best, especially on those days when they don't quite feel like it. I'm a living witness!

Learn, Know, and Be True to You

The greatest personal development you can hope to achieve begins with self-awareness. How self-aware are you really? Remember, 95% of people say they are self-aware, but only 10 -15% actually are.[10] One of the first areas you will need to develop to become true to yourself and others is in the area of emotional intelligence. While I strongly recommend that you engage in a more detailed emotional intelligence assessment, you can begin by realistically doing some self-introspection and answering my top eight emotional intelligence awareness questions here.

1) AUTHENTICITY

How often are you vulnerable enough to show up as your authentic self?

Do you pretend to be someone else? Is the "fake it until you make it" line of reasoning your go-to in every situation? Do you lack confidence or struggle with imposter syndrome? Do you find yourself being a people pleaser or trying to conform to a preconceived notion of who you think others believe you should be or behaving how others believe you should behave? When you show up as your authentic self and are willing to be vulnerable with your faults or insecurities, it subconsciously gives others

---

[10] Kauflin, Jeff. "Only 15% of People Are Self-Aware -- Here's How to Change." Forbes Magazine, 29 June 2017, www.forbes.com/sites/jef-fkauflin/2017/05/10/only-15-of-people-are-self-aware-heres-how-to-change/?sh=1d4e48df2b8c.

permission to be authentic as well. It's easier to understand others when they walk in their truth. It is also easier for them to understand you.

2) FEELINGS

How cognizant and interpretive are you of your feelings?

Can you adequately explain your feelings? (Example, some people might say they are "mad" when they are really "frustrated," "annoyed," "confused," or "emotionally hurt.") Can you recognize and identify with those same feelings in others? When you can adequately interpret your feelings, you have a better chance of understanding and connecting with others. You will have greater insight or empathy into the decisions they make and what motivates them to act.

3) THOUGHTS

How well do you control your thoughts?

Do you think about what you are going to say before you say it? Do you delay your responses to take in other perspectives and formulate your best responses or reactions, especially in conflict, or do you emotionally blurt out the first thing on your mind? Can you be authentic with your feelings but intentionally choose your thoughts about them? Do you stew on negative thoughts, allowing them to control your disposition and actions? How you think determines what you say and how you act, and to others you are what you say and what you do. So, think about what you think about.

4) WORDS

How often do your words hurt rather than help or heal?

Do you often or even sometimes say things that you know hurt others' feelings in an attempt to get it off your chest, give them a piece of your mind, or whip them into shape? Do you find yourself in self-criticism because you did not use your words empathically or you avoided using your words to respond at all? Finding the right words to communicate in a helpful manner is the key to connection, collaboration, and motivation.

The more you grow your vocabulary and empathic communication skills, the greater your chances to make desired connections with others.

5) APOLOGIZING

How hard is it for you to say, "I'm sorry?"

Do you believe that as the leader you can't apologize because others will think you are stupid, incompetent, or weak? Can you remember the last time you sincerely apologized? What did you say when you did, and how effective was it? How did it make you feel? If apologizing is hard for you, you may need to undergo an uncomfortable but necessary ego check with humility. Realize that having the sincerity and ability to apologize doesn't make you a weaker leader or person. In fact, it makes you stronger. Being vulnerable and honest with others when you make a mistake demonstrates the humility that draws people to you (especially SINCERITY S-Motivated). It opens the door for others to feel comfortable admitting their mistakes as well.

6) FORGIVENESS

How likely are you to forgive others?

Are you still carrying a grudge today for something that happened a long time ago? Do you still judge someone's capabilities today for mistakes they made in the past? How long do you remain upset or angry when people disappoint you? Leaders should quickly realize we are all human, and with that comes a boatload of mistakes and fallacies. That is not just emotional intelligence but intelligence period. Forgiveness does NOT mean you must be a doormat or pushover for the bad actors of the world. Nor does it mean you are naïve. It means you are both empathic and wise enough to discern when someone is sincerely sorry for their mistakes, words, or behaviors, and when they are focused on growing, healing, or moving ahead in a positive manner. It also frees your spirit so you can operate from a place of healing and authenticity rather than fear or hurt.

7) SERVICE

How much do you care about helping others?

How committed are you to help others in need? How much do you desire to see others succeed? Do you go above and beyond to make the assist? Do you identify as well as serve others' needs? Do you set aside time to ask or talk about ways you can help? Good leaders help others in need. Emotionally intelligent leaders understand situations and others' needs so well they often identify and implement ways to be of service before help is even needed. This is next-level servant leadership, and you know you have arrived in a great space of emotional intelligence when you can care and serve to this degree.

8) FEEDBACK

How well do you honestly manage and offer criticism and praise?

Do you both give and receive criticism as constructive, or do you harp on the more destructive aspects? Do you take action to demonstrate what you have learned from criticism? Do you give praise when it is due and in a manner that it will be best received? Do you find it hard to give or receive a compliment? Can you receive praise with humility? How often do you feel comfortable making suggestions? Do evaluation meetings often make you anxious? How sensitive are you to other's ability to receive criticism or praise? The mindset of being improved vs. approved is important here, and you need a good degree of emotional intelligence to keep this at the forefront of both offering and receiving feedback.

Taking the time to be honest with yourself is critical for tapping into the self-awareness desperately needed in leadership. This book has been dedicated to helping leaders understand the six key motivators to help engage others in the workplace. However, I would be remiss if we did not address that leadership begins with understanding yourself first. Think of it like the airline theory of putting on your own oxygen mask before you assist another. You cannot give what you do not have. So, kudos to you for doing the work in the gymnasium of self-awareness. You are getting stronger already, building the emotionally intelligent muscles needed to flex and win with others!

Learn, Know, and Be True to Others

A 2022 Gallup poll had a relevant finding as it pertains to leaders and engagement. They found that 70% of the variance in a team's engagement is related to their management. Some argued that employees should be self-motivated and accountable for their own engagement, not emotionally coddled by their leadership. However, when trying to determine who is most responsible for employee engagement, the survey determined managers do indeed create the conditions that promote the behaviors of engaged employees (or just the opposite) with the relationships they establish. Thus, it suggested the "manager is either an engagement-creating coach or an engagement-destroying boss, but both relationships affect employee behavior."[11]

In other words, employees believe their engagement, or lack thereof, is primarily your (the leader's) responsibility or fault. We evaluate leadership more for relationships than for results because the results are based on relationships and not the other way around. The more you are playing that game of catch with the individuals on your team, and the more you empathically know not just their orientation and needs, but also their motivation, the greater and more consistent the success.

At this point, you should have a firm grasp on how you can play catch with everyone. It begins with asking questions and actively listening to empathically understand which Leadership 6-S Motivators and principles are at play. To recap, all six motivators exist to some degree in virtually everyone in workplace culture. That's why learning them all is fundamental. Doing the work to learn the specific motivators that drive each team member is where you will use emotional intelligence to grow your most productive relationships and results.

Because I am empathic and believe in providing SOLUTIONS, I've created a short reference or cheat sheet to help you remain cognizant and

---

[11] Royal, Ken. "Who's Responsible for Employee Engagement." Gallup.Com, 29 Apr. 2022, www.gallup.com/workplace/266822/engaged-employees-differently.aspx.

present in the empathic leadership mindset. It is a brief "To Think or To Do" list to help stimulate each of these motivators in your people. It includes a straightforward way for you to remember how you can work through the emotions to "play catch," or affectively communicate.

SIGNIFICANCE – Help others see how they matter; (I GOT IT!); encourage creativity and highlight unique and valued contributions and skillsets; empower each team member to have a voice even if they don't have a vote; show genuine appreciation, concern, and respect, not just for what a person does but for who they are. *Significance is at its best when people experience the inherent rewards of using their skills for a purpose of service.*

The Catch: "Help me see how I matter."

SECURITY – Show faith, not fear; demonstrate a mindset and actions of resilience; be sensitive to financial and flexibility needs and the importance of resources and benefits; offer consistent, constructive feedback; speak of future plans, vision, and opportunities; encourage innovation; provide adequate resources to complete tasks; manage from and encourage open mindedness and approachability; allow freedom to fly (and freedom to fail); provide a culture of stability and control without micromanaging or dictatorship. **Security is at its best when communicated with integrity, confidence, and empathy.**

The Catch: "Help me feel safe."

SOLUTIONS – Demonstrate knowledge; don't shrink from problems; involve your team in problem solving strategies; stimulate critical thinking and outside the box perspectives; welcome adverse opinions and ideas without intimidation; test biases; encourage research and resourcefulness; resolve problems quickly but without rushing to judgement; avoid complaining and celebrating the problem; welcome challenges that stimulate growth; be firm in decision making; motivate and inspire for the win. **Solutions are best stimulated with appreciation for and recognition of diverse cultures, styles, intelligence, and ideas.**

The Catch: "Help me help us work smarter."

STRUCTURE – Begin with clarity of vision, mission, plans, duties, and rules; deliver organized processes and logistics; commit to a strong foundation of accomplishing tasks with sensible systems; prioritize innovation and exploration; build and implement new ideas with facts and data; be consistent; set boundaries but never limits; proactively communicate and collaborate; strategize to strengths; define expectations clearly upfront; follow up! *Structure is best provided with the endgame in mind, and buy-in from all involved at heart.*

The Catch: "Help me feel organized, steady, and ready."

SINCERITY – Listen empathically; speak truthfully; be true to your team but also be true to yourself; prioritize integrity; cultivate quality relationships, products, and service; understand trust is continuously earned and easily burned; promptly apologize for mistakes or misunderstandings; be authentic; be clear; be transparent; be humble; encourage integrity, loyalty, and authenticity in others with your leadership example. *Sincerity is best communicated when intentions are humble and clear, and words and actions align.*

The Catch: "Help me live and work in truth."

SELFLESSNESS – Humble yourself with a service-first heart; communicate based on "The Catch;" be the example of going above and beyond; always consider the greater good—what's best for the team; foster a culture of diversity, equity, inclusion, and belonging; proactively seek collaboration ventures; share ideas without fear of losing the credit.

Selflessness is best remembered as this: If you think it's all about you, soon you'll be right, because 'you' is all you will have.

The Catch: "Help me feel that I belong and that WE are a team."

The Final Case Study

Wow! With the help of Ricky, a few good stories, a bunch of case studies, and some emotional intelligence theory, assessments, principles, and practices, we've covered a lot! It's now time for you to create your own Leadership 6-S story. What case studies will go into a book about your Empathic Leadership Success? How will you help others to feel **SIGNIFICANT** and **SECURE** in their roles? What **SOLUTIONS** and **STRUCTURE** will you develop, encourage, and implement? What acts of **SINCERITY** and **SELFLESSNESS** will define your culture and leadership efforts? Whatever the plan, you have the tools to create a story that highlights how your empathy helped motivate your followers to grow and succeed despite adversity. I doubt your story will be about how power and intimidation got people to do what you needed them to do. Nor will it be a story about lack of employee engagement or a case study about how you gave up because leadership was too hard.

Your story will be about a leader who has learned to focus on being improved rather than approved, and whose leadership by empathic example helps others do the same. Your story will depict an intelligent leader who has carefully discerned that people don't care how much you know until they know how much you care. That knowledge goes beyond simply knowing people's orientation and needs, but also what deeply motivates them to engage and act, especially in times of challenge. Because of the focus on these things, your story will be about an empathic leader who uses six key motivators to help keep a department, team, or organization unified and productive towards service, significance, and purpose. That leader has gone from good to great, and empathy was the best teacher of how to love and to lead. I can see it all clearly. Can you?

Finally, I can't help but smile when I not only see this confident and successful leader, but also hear them yell, "I GOT IT!" That is a story of "6-S!"

Appendix A

6-S Values Sort Exercise

The following is a list of 24 Common Workplace Values

1. Assess the degree of importance each of the 24 values holds for you. Place the corresponding letter identifying your value assessment next to each listed value.
2. Identify and star (*) your top 12 Values (These will likely be your A and B – Always or Often Valued selections.)
3. After condensing your list to 12, go back and circle/highlight only your *top 6 core values.*

A. Always Valued   **B. Often Valued**   **C. Sometimes Valued**
D. Seldom Valued   **E. Never Valued**

_______1.   **Achievement** – A sense of accomplishment, mastery, completion or exceeding of goals.

_______2.   **Aesthetics** – An appreciation of the beauty of things, ideas, surroundings, personal space, etc.

_______3.   **Autonomy** – Self-sufficiency; self-reliance. Ability to act independently and make most decisions and choices.

_______4.   **Balance** – Giving proper weight to each area of a person's life. A sense of life-stability and completeness.

_______5.   **Challenge** – Continually facing complex and demanding tasks and problems. Thrill for problem solving.

_______6.   **Change/Variety** – Absence of routine. Participating in new or different work or activities. Spontaneity.

_______7.   **Collaboration** – Having close, cooperative working relations with other individuals, team, or group.

_______8.   **Competence** – Demonstrating a high degree of proficiency, knowledge, efficiency, or effectiveness.

_______9.   **Competition** – Rivalry or challenge with winning as the goal.

_____10. **Courage** – Willingness to have a voice or take action to stand up for one's beliefs.

_____11. **Creativity** – Discovering, developing, or designing new or unique concepts using innovation and imagination.

_____12. **Economic Security** – Steady and secure employment/income. Financial gain, reward or stability. Low risk.

_____13. **Enjoyment** – Fun, joy, and laughter; having a sense of pleasantness, amusement, gratitude.

_____14. **Family** – Spending time with spouse, children, parents, siblings, or extended family members.

_____15. **Helping Others** – Helping others attain their goals. Providing care and support.

_____16. **Influence** – Having an impact or effect on the attitudes or opinions of others. The power of persuasion.

_____17. **Integrity** – Acting in accord with moral and ethical standards. Honesty, sincerity, truth, trustworthiness.

_____18. **Loyalty** – Faithfulness, duty, dedication.

_____19. **Order** – Respectful of authority, rules, regulations. A sense of stability, routine, predictability.

_____20. **Personal Development** – Dedication to maximizing one's potential. An appreciation or desire for growth.

_____21. **Recognition** – Positive feedback and public credit for work well done. Respect and admiration.

_____22. **Reflection** – Taking time out to think about the past, present, and future.

_____23. **Self-Respect** – Pride, self-esteem, sense of personal identity.

_____24. **Spirituality** – Strong spiritual or religious beliefs. Moral fulfillment.

Appendix B

6-S Perceptions Survey

1. Identify a total of six people in your social circles as follows:
    - Confidantes: Two people who are in your closest or most intimate inner circle. These are people you trust and who you feel you share tight personal connections with. You believe these people know you best. (Ex: Spouse, sibling, parent, best friend, etc.)
    - Casuals: Two people who you would consider to be on a more casual friendship connection with you. You believe these people know you reasonably well. (Friend, work buddy, coach or mentor, social connection, etc.)
    - Acquaintances: Two people who you consider to be more distant social connections. These are people you know, but not well. (New work colleague, church or group associate, client, etc.)

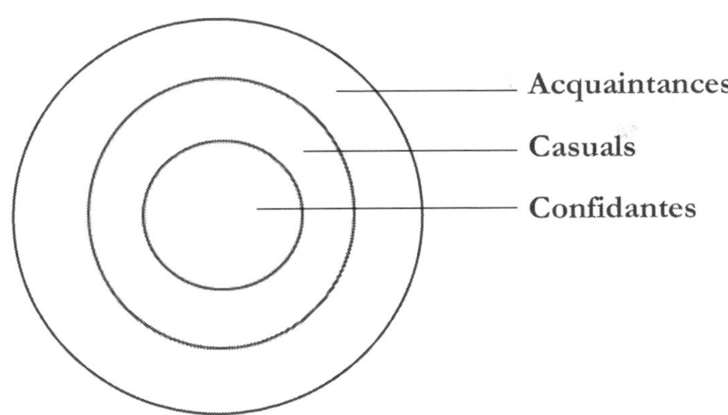

2. Ask each person in each of the categories to describe your character (non-physical attributes) as best as possible using only four adjectives or descriptors (i.e. warm-hearted, humorous, opinionated, talkative, etc.).

3. Advise them you are participating in a perceptions survey and that their descriptors are not a "fishing for compliments expedition." You want their truest perceptions to include less-favorable descriptors if they have them. Also advise them to offer the first four descriptors that come to mind and not to overthink it.

4. List out each person's responses on a grid or table so that you can easily view them collectively.

5. What commonalities do you notice? Are they similar in the same circles but different in others? Can you discern why? Are they similar across all circles? What big picture does this paint of how you are perceived? How do these responses relate to how you see yourself? How do they relate to your values? What do you find surprising? In what ways do you desire to be perceived differently? (Consider not only what was said, but what wasn't.)

References

Brower, Tracy. "Empathy Is the Most Important Leadership Skill According to Research." *Forbes Magazine*, 12 Sept. 2021, www.forbes.com/sites/tracybrower/2021/09/19/empathy-is-the-most-important-leadership-skill-according-to-research/?sh=7d9ae2313dc5.

Goleman, Daniel, et al. *Primal Leadership: Learning to Lead with Emotional Intelligence*. Harvard Business Review Press, 2004.

Jones, Vera. *Now I See: A Journey of Prophecy, Pain, and Purpose*. Outskirts Press, 2019.

Kauflin, Jeff. "Only 15% of People Are Self-Aware -- Here's How to Change." *Forbes Magazine*, 29 June 2017, www.forbes.com/sites/jeffkauflin/2017/05/10/only-15-of-people-are-self-aware-heres-how-to-change/?sh=1d4e48df2b8c.

Laker, Benjamin. "Every Leader Can Benefit from Coaching. Here's Why." *Forbes Magazine*, 4 Oct. 2022, www.forbes.com/sites/benjaminlaker/2022/10/04/every-leader-can-benefit-from-coaching-heres-why/.

"National Institute for Occupational Safety & Health." *Centers for Disease Control and Prevention*, 1 Sept. 2023, www.cdc.gov/niosh/.

Royal, Ken. "Who's Responsible for Employee Engagement." *Gallup.Com*, 29 Apr. 2022, www.gallup.com/workplace/266822/engaged-employees-differently.aspx.

Sweeney, Erica. "Most Americans Living Paycheck to Paycheck This Year, Survey Finds." *Investopedia,* 18 Sept. 2023, www.investopedia.com/most-americans-report-living-paycheck-to-paycheck-new-survey-finds-7970611.

"Workplace Conflict Statistics 2023: Pollack Peacebuilding." *Pollack Peacebuilding Systems,* 1 Dec. 2023, pollackpeacebuilding.com/workplace-conflict-statistics/.

About the Author

 **Vera Jones** is a motivational speaker, author, coach, retired 30-year TV & radio broadcasting veteran, and Syracuse University Hall-of-Fame Scholar-Athlete. She is most widely known for her women's basketball analysis and reporting for various networks, including ESPN, Fox Sports, Madison Square Garden Network, NBA-TV, and the Big Ten Network. Vera holds a master's degree from Syracuse University's Newhouse School of Communications where she first developed her interest in the psychology of interpersonal communication. A brief stint with the Paul Robeson Performing Arts Company, combined with her time as a standup comedienne, add variety, humor, and depth to her communication and presentation endeavors.

In 2008, Vera founded Vera's VoiceWorks, LLC, a motivational speaking and professional development training entity based in Jacksonville, FL. As a Mediation Training Institute (MTI) Certified Mediator, a Trainer in Workplace Conflict Resolution, and University of North Florida Professor of Public Speaking, Vera uses her empathic communication gifts to inspire, coach, and develop others through various leadership and professional development training forums. Vera is honored and humbled to have become a Hall of Fame inductee with the Boys & Girls Club of America Alumni (2023) and the National Association of Women Business Owners (NAWBO 2022). A native of Prince George's County, MD, Vera resides in the sunshine and warmth of Jacksonville, FL.

Engage With Empathy!
Get the Leadership 6-S Training!

With Gallup reporting a whopping 67% of American workers identified as "disengaged" or unhappy at work, organizations are finding greater truth in the adage, "They don't care how much you know until they know how much you care." In light of this, Vera Jones has written the book and designed the Leadership 6-S coaching program to help leaders learn and develop the 6-S Motivators that help them connect, communicate, and collaborate with greater EMPATHY.

More Books from Vera Jones

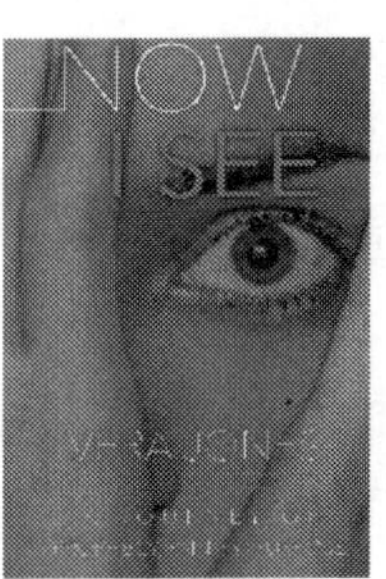

Play Through the Foul: Basketball Lessons for the Game of Life (VoiceWorks Media, 2009)

Now I See: A Journey of Prophecy, Pain, and Purpose (Outskirts Press, 2019)

New Best Friend: A Little Book of Faith (Karen Hunter Media, LLC, 2011)

www.verasvoiceworks.com

SCAN ME